'Full of entertaining stories, personality and a healthy sprinkling of stats, *Networking for Introverts* is a manual for winning business in today's economy, and I would recommend it to anyone who wants to grow their client base. *Networking for Introverts* is brimming with great advice and inspiration, and is the kind of book you will read and then go back to time and again for tips'
— **Annette King, CEO, Publicis Groupe UK**

'*Networking for Introverts* fizzes with actionable ideas. A firecracker of a book to get you blazing a trail for new business from two of the best operators around'
— **Julia Hobsbawm OBE, founder and chair, Editorial Intelligence, and author of the bestselling** *The Simplicity Principle*

'A must-read — especially post-Covid — for anyone involved in business generation. Entertaining whilst it educates, this indispensable guidebook is a revelation for any driven professional and will definitely put you ahead of the competition — if she hasn't read it as well. Time excellently well spent'
— **Jane Reeve, Chief Communications Officer, Ferrari**

'Humour is one of the only things that increases when you share it, as the authors of this immensely good-natured book on the human touch in business know. But I also found myself thinking about plumbing metaphors. May the good Lord spare us from pipeline accelerators, but here you can read and understand how in business, as in life, it's better to be a radiator than a drain'
— **Stephen Bayley, recovering design guru and** author of *Value: What money can't buy.* *andbook for practical hedonism*

'An enjoyable and practical asset recommended to anyone who has to develop new business. It nails what it takes to find new clients and be a valued, trusted advisor to them; helping others helps us be more successful'
— **Guy Gregory, Executive Director, Client Care and Business Development, CBRE Ltd**

'Accelerate your understanding of how to grow business, fast. Recommended to anyone who dreads networking events: an entertaining and effective guide to oiling the wheels of business without the need to be oleaginous'
— **Sophie Devonshire, CEO, The Marketing Society**

'An extremely timely book. Now more than ever we need to understand how to communicate with each other better'
— **Rachel Bridge, author of *Already Brilliant* and *How to Work for Yourself***

'Such a refreshing book about such a necessary part of doing business, and something so often misunderstood. *Networking for Introverts* is a thoroughly enjoyable and helpful read, packed with great examples, stories and tools for how to develop business, and, above all, packed with common sense. And all expressed in a natural and jargon-free way too. Terrific stuff'
— **Rita Clifton CBE, portfolio chair and non-executive director**

LOUISA CLARKE   DAVID KEAN

Networking
for
INTROVERTS

PIATKUS

PIATKUS

First published as *Catalyst* in Great Britain in 2021 by Piatkus
This paperback edition published in 2025 by Piatkus

13 5 7 9 10 8 6 4 2

A CIP catalogue record for this book
is available from the British Library.

ISBN: 978-0-349-42917-5

Typeset in Bembo by Hewer Text UK Ltd, Edinburgh
Printed and bound in Great Britain by Clays Ltd, Elcograf S.p.A.

Papers used by Piatkus are from well-managed forests and other responsible sources.

Piatkus
An imprint of
Little, Brown Book Group
Carmelite House
50 Victoria Embankment
London EC4Y 0DZ

The authorised representative
in the EEA is
Hachette Ireland
8 Castlecourt Centre, Dublin 15, D15
XTP3, Ireland
(email: info@hbgi.ie)

An Hachette UK Company
www.hachette.co.uk

www.littlebrown.co.uk

To Nick, Joseph, Michael — FF.

For my darling Tanyushka, who thought I was only networking.
Your David.

CONTENTS

PREFACE

THIS BOOK WILL CHANGE YOUR LIFE

'The meeting of two personalities is like the
contact of two chemical substances: if there
is any reaction, both are transformed.'
Carl Jung

Why this book now? Because now, like never before, we need to
be better at business generation: in the brave new world that the
COVID-19 pandemic has thrown at us, we need to create all the
opportunity we can to rebuild our businesses again. Increasing
the number of clients and customers we attract has never been
more vital. Those businesses that do it well will survive, even
thrive. Those that do not generate new business, or do not do it
as well as their competitors, will simply go to the wall. Many
have already. This is a brutally testing time for our skills and
abilities.

But as we adjust to the new environment, as we climb out of
lockdown, as we restart the economic engine of commerce
nationally and internationally, one thing above all others will
differentiate the successful: the ability to generate new business
actively and deliberately rather than haphazardly and by chance.
Now, more than ever before, the skills and techniques for getting
new customers and clients through our doors – virtual or otherwise – is the single most important factor in personal and

corporate survival. We have written this book to help as many people as possible do it well and so regrow their personal prosperity, their enterprises and our economy.

Why are we qualified to write this book? We love business development. We love prospecting for new clients. We love networking and meeting strangers. We, it seems, love all the things that many other people absolutely hate. We have spent our careers helping people to feel the same way about these three things as we do. This book is our attempt to persuade you – the stranger we haven't met yet – that business development, and all the stuff associated with it, is not only too important to put in the 'I don't like it' box, but that it can also be great fun, very rewarding and, actually, isn't that hard to do very well. Like anything in life, if you know how to do it properly, and you are willing to practise it a bit, you will start to enjoy it. And if you start to enjoy it, you will start to do it better and better. And as you do it better and better, you will win more and more new business, make more and more contacts, enjoy their company more and so create a virtuous circle that will last you your entire lifetime. Sounds like we're promising to change your life, doesn't it? We are, especially if this economic situation has rocked you and your business to its foundations.

Let's start by looking at why people hate all this stuff so viscerally, because nowadays no one can afford to hate new business generation – it's not a luxury anyone can afford anymore. There is a lot of rubbish written about new business. It has been turned into a management discipline full of dreadful jargon, an enterprise plagued with overcomplication, characterised by words and phrases that are designed to dress it up as mechanistic, rational and precise. Here are some examples: 'systemic prospecting', 'Customer Relationship Management (CRM)', 'data capture', 'relationship audit', 'pipeline acceleration', 'bizmeth', 'conversion ratio optimisation' and 'business transformation'.

These words make it all sound very grown-up, automated even – as if just by pulling the right levers in the right sequence, you will win.

As if that wasn't enough, 'business development' doesn't have a very positive reputation. It is a synonym for selling – that dreaded activity many people distrust so much. It is perceived to be the domain of the slick, the 'super-closers' – fast-talking, gift-of-the-gab merchants who can sell ice to the Inuit. People who pride themselves on being able to clinch the deal at the last minute, spot an opportunity and – *bang!* – close that sale! People think of business developers (salespeople), as being red-in-tooth-and-claw, sharks, the wolves of Wall Street. They think of them as people who don't care what they are selling; they're just enjoying the next 'kill'. Predatory, old-school, foot-in-the-door charlatans. Latter-day snake-oil sellers. This is what springs to mind for most people when they think of selling or business development. You'd be forgiven for wanting to run a mile from them.

As for networking, well, don't get us started. The dreaded 'networking' event. The thing so many people have to be forced to attend. An evening of drinking lukewarm white wine and making small talk in the company of strangers, most of whom seem to be enviably adept networkers as they flit between different groups, spreading bonhomie and sunshine to all. Whilst we, the proverbial wallflowers, scan the room desperately searching for the friendly face of anyone we vaguely know, so we can attach to them like a limpet for the rest of the event and avoid having to meet anyone new. Yes, *that* kind of networking. It doesn't *have* to be a taxi ride home filled with relief that you escaped without being spotted leaving, and the self-congratulatory feeling that you have done your duty for another month – even though you met absolutely no one new all night.

There is another way.

In writing a book about business development, networking and prospecting, we have taken two problems head-on. Firstly, we have taken on the prejudice held by many professional people that business development is a dirty, vulgar activity and that chasing new clients isn't something reputable companies should have to do. Secondly, we have taken on the task of unwrapping the layers of jargon and management-speak that have wrapped themselves around what is actually a very simple human activity: the thrill of the chase.

When we started in this discipline, one colleague summed the first problem up when, on meeting David, who was the company's first business development director, he exclaimed: 'Oh, you're the agency tart then!' 'Tart' is a rather old-fashioned synonym for prostitute. A little earlier in his career, while still a very junior employee at another London firm that was losing clients daily, David made a presentation to the owner advocating that the company actively chase new clients to replace those that were leaving. He spoke about how to do this and about professionalising and resourcing the discipline of new business – something unheard of at the time. At the end of his presentation, David peered to the back of the room and waited for the owner to give his verdict. The verdict was two words:

'How *vulgar*.'

The company went into liquidation five months later, costing 324 jobs. This attitude, sadly, still permeates many professions. Whilst many companies have reluctantly created a new business function, it is often staffed with administrators who are unqualified in the industry they represent (law, architecture, real estate, etc.), and so get ignored or sidelined by the practitioners, who dismiss them as second-class citizens.

Jargon and management speak are also dangerous. A lot of books on the subject of business development, a lot of courses taught by business schools, and a lot of training companies selling proprietary business development techniques have vested interests in maintaining the edifice of pseudo-scientific complexity that has been built up around business development. There's too much academic textbook theory out there and not enough down-to-earth practical simplicity to show how it is really done in the real world.

We will expose this conspiracy of nonsense. It is important to demystify the thrill of the chase so that more people in more businesses can do it better and see that it is not scary or underhand, that it doesn't require vast computer databases, a plethora of processes, armies of functionaries or the gift of the gab in order to do it brilliantly. All it requires is a willingness to try new things, a bit of bravery, some simple techniques, a bit of preparation, thoughtfulness, practice and the self-discipline to keep going. Basic business, basic human qualities.

Business development is not about mechanics. It is not about pulling levers. Nor is it about pulling the wool over people's eyes. It is far subtler than that and much more fun. Business development is about catalysing relationships – creating connections between human beings that change worlds. We suspect that professionals clothe business development in the language of management because it makes it seem precise, quantifiable, ordered and scientific, and to make it sound macho for the old-school sales types. Management speak makes business development sound both controllable and dynamic, all about closing ratios and hard financial outcomes. In reality, it is organic and unpredictable. Business development is more about chemistry than mathematics or physics. Business development is about speeding up change. It is about changing people's circumstances, changing their decisions, changing their partners, changing their suppliers, changing their skills, changing their outcomes, changing their performance, changing their fortunes. It is the art of transforming the most volatile and unpredictable compound in the universe – human beings – from their current state into a new one. And the catalyst for that change is you.

We use the idea of a catalyst throughout this book because the catalytic process best describes our view about the role of the business generator, prospector and networker. A catalyst is an agent that is added to a process to make a chemical reaction happen more quickly, without changing the catalyst itself. Our job as a business development catalyst is to be a person whose talk, enthusiasm and energy causes others to be more friendly, enthusiastic and energetic in response. This is the realm of personal chemical reactions: the emotion that two people get when they share a special connection, when they develop a rapport. We are in the business of catalysing the impulse in another person to feel *I need to see this person again*, because they feel that we 'click'. By getting this reaction, we create a landscape of endless opportunities. This is the genesis of all successful networking and new business work. It is the foundation upon which every other conversation is built. Do this right, keep it reacting positively, and new business will come. Do this right and your world will change for the better.

This book will lay bare the best ways to catalyse better human relationships and win more profitable new business. Using a combination of illustrative anecdotes, hard-won experience and step-by-step recommendations, we demystify the science and art of business development to help you *enjoy* it as well as do it more effectively. If we do that, and we help you become a catalyst too, we will have achieved what we set out to do – which really is to change your life and to extend the life of your business.

PART I

CATALYST: WHY AND HOW TO BE ONE

CHAPTER 1

BEING A CATALYTIC CONVERTER

'Energy begets energy'
Dolly Parton

If you are genuinely good at what you do, you can help people. If you are in the business of client service – and you are, whether you sell cars, power plants, biscuits, fine dining, financial services or education – you have a mission to help as many people as possible.

So why would you leave it to fate to see who turns up at your front door asking for help? Why wouldn't you want to spread the word, evangelise, make it your business to help as many people as you can? Why keep your brilliance to yourself?

The more new business you win, the more your reputation grows. The more new business you win, the 'hotter' you become. Not only do you attract more clients, but you also attract the best talent in your industry and you work on the most interesting problems. You have more opportunities to exercise your skills across the widest possible canvas and you create a virtuous circle of success. More new business begets more new business. It attracts higher-calibre talent and more interesting work, which in turn generates the accolades and awards within your industry, and feeds your reputation for being the best. That reputation gives you another advantage – when you are in open pitch for a new client, your competition is mentally one–nil down knowing they are up against the very best player in the industry who is also at the top of their game.

It is also important because your clients will want to hear what you have to say, and you can charge them more for the privilege. They will listen to you because they know that your advice or product or service is sought by many others whom they probably respect. They will be willing to pay a premium because they know you can pick and choose who you deal with.

To illustrate this, we need to introduce a friend of ours. He is a mediator – a qualified solicitor who helps adjudicate disputes between parties so they can be settled without spending time and money in the legal courts. Let's call him Mike. Mike told us a story about a trip he took to St Ives, a picture-perfect fishing town on the north coast of Cornwall. Despite its beauty, St Ives is situated on one of the most perilous coastlines in Britain. The indigenous population is close-knit and trades are passed on from one generation to the next. As in all coastal communities around Britain, the local heroes are the lifeboat crews – members of the Royal National Lifeboat Institute, the RNLI. Every one of them is a volunteer and every one of them keeps good their promise to turn out to help any boat or person in distress at sea, whatever the weather and at whatever risk to their own life and limb.

Mike was going down to St Ives to mediate a dispute between a local boat owner and the coxswain of the lifeboat. On its launch down the ramp from the lifeboat station one day, the lifeboat had glanced a blow to a small pleasure boat anchored to a buoy in the harbour. It wasn't a malicious act; it was just an accident. The collision had caused some damage to the pleasure craft and the owner was threatening to sue the lifeboat coxswain for the cost of repairs. Our friend had agreed to meet the plaintiff in a pub down by the quayside. It was a sunny lunchtime and they took a pint and a table outside in the pub's front garden. After a few pleasantries, Mike asked the pleasure boat owner if they could see his home from where they were sitting.

'Absolutely,' he replied. 'Can you see that row of cottages halfway up the hill? My house is the second from the end of that row – the one with the white front door.'

'It looks beautiful. Must have a fine view over the seafront and the harbour?' observed our friend.

'Yes – that was why we bought it, for the view.'

'And what's it like living in a Cornish fishing village?'

'We retired here two years ago. It takes a while for people to get used to you but now they all know we're living here and not just using it as a second home for holidays, people are pretty friendly and welcoming. It's a real community – they're all pretty tight with one another.'

'And tell me,' continued our friend, genuinely curious, 'I think I can see you have a little garden gate and wall that separates your house from the street. How far is it from the front window to the little wall with the front gate in it?'

'Oh, I'd say it's about twenty feet,' replied the man.

'The reason I ask,' continued Mike, 'is because, if you continue with your legal action against the local lifeboat, in a town where everyone knows everyone else, and where the lifeboat crew are the local heroes, you're going to get a brick through your front window from a friendly local who might have had one drink too many on a Friday night. You're not going to be too popular round here, are you? Is it worth it? Wouldn't it be better if we could just come to a private arrangement and you drop the charges? If we can all climb down from our high horses for a minute, I'm sure we could sort something out.'

The plaintiff could see the sense in what our friend advised. When the coxswain arrived at the pub a little later, he was able to apologise for the accident, offer to help repair the boat and they were able to settle things amicably and enjoy their pints. And our friend walked off £10,000 better off for a day's work sitting in the sunshine helping two people who had got stuck. He had been worth listening to because he not only knew the law but he could think laterally to apply his understanding to the specific situation. And he had earned his money – a considerable fee for a day's work – because he had saved his clients much more than £10,000 if the case had gone to court and because he had enabled peace to prevail in a small community whilst allowing both parties to save face.

In telling you this tale, we have positioned our friend, Mike, as a sagacious dispenser of wisdom and as a counsellor to the troubled. Which is exactly what he did every time he shared this funny story with people – and he did this a lot. (We will be hearing more about Mike later on. He was a consummate catalyst.) His story illustrates better than any case study could his skill at steering through potentially choppy waters towards an elegant solution. Wouldn't you want such a skilful operator in your corner?

Think of the best work you have done. Think of how you can bring it alive as a story so it illustrates how you do what you do, not in a trumpet-blowy, self-aggrandising way, but as an amusing tale, a good yarn. Underpinning all the best stories is a moral – in this case it was 'think of the long game, of where your interests truly lie'. For the cottage owner in St Ives, his interests would be best served by keeping a friendly relationship with the lifeboat. How can you show that what you do is done in a way that helps people take better decisions or act in a way that serves their own interests cleverly? A story is so much more persuasive than a case study or a page full of facts or statistics.

After a presentation, 63 per cent of attendees remember stories. Only 5 per cent remember statistics.

(Obviously, only 5 per cent of you will remember this statistic.) That's why this book is full of stories and not statistics. Statistics are useful if used judiciously, and if they have the wow factor. But a blizzard of stats do not build a relationship. 100 per cent true. 100 per cent ignored in every single business presentation made around the planet.

THE CATALYST MODEL

There are a plethora of sales models out there – just Google 'pipeline development models' and watch them all come up. They all make logical sense, and they all extoll rational business acquisition processes which might help you. But, with very few exceptions, they all omit the single quality that will make your pipeline actually work. They leave out the key ingredient: human likeability. The emotional connection you catalyse with the person you are in discussion with – how they feel about you and how you treat them. The chemistry between you both. Whether or not you 'click'. There are many entirely legitimate pipeline models in existence which show the progression of a prospect through the sales funnel to the final stage – purchase. Far too often these models are built on an understanding of the prospect customer or client as an entirely rational being, making an 'educated' purchase decision. For example, one picked at random from the many on the market:

> 'The sales rep will convert the lead into a customer if they are able to answer with authority the questions in the sales funnel and convey the match between the lead's problem and the rep's proposed solution.'

In other words, providing you – the sales representative mentioned above – have taken the prospect through all the preceding rational steps, if you answer their final questions, the sale will be yours. Hoorah!

Really?

We do not live in a rational world. People do not, in the vast majority of cases, buy rationally. The behavioural economist, adman and TED speaker, Rory Sutherland, has written a brilliant book called *Alchemy: The surprising power of ideas that don't make sense** that demonstrates this beautifully. He factors in something he calls 'psycho-logic', and demonstrates with myriad examples how logic does not apply in solving so many problems where human beings are involved, especially their buying decisions. Thank heavens they don't; it gives all business developers a fair chance. If logic rather than psycho-logic was all that mattered, most businesses wouldn't be in business very long. People may *justify* their purchase rationally, and rationality will probably have played a significant role in the purchase process, but more often than not, it boils down to whether they *like and trust* the person they are buying from. Whether or not you have made them feel that you are genuinely interested in helping them over the entire length of the purchase cycle, however long that cycle lasts. This is what an old client of ours describes as being a 'diligent farmer' – a person who patiently tends his crops, looks after them, nurtures them, feeds them, waters them, is there for them through hail, storm, snow and sunshine and brings in a bountiful harvest through consistent, daily care of every living thing on his farm.

The diligent farmer

Diligent farmers are the best model for business developers to adopt. They work consistently. They never slack. They shepherd

* Rory Sutherland, *Alchemy: The surprising power of ideas that don't make sense* (London: WH Allen, 2019).

their flock and steer them from danger. They invest care and attention on each and every one of their charges. Their interests are best served by serving others' interests brilliantly and, when the time comes, they reap the benefits. Their fortunes depend on creating strong long-term relationships with their customers and producing, every time, a consistently brilliant product, year after year. In return, their customers are there for them year after year. The diligent farmer's methodology requires huge effort but it works and it is rewarding. There is always a market for diligent farmers.

Be a diligent farmer with your network. Don't be an amateur, part-time gardener, only out in sunshine rather than in all weathers; and don't be a pesticide farmer, managing all your relationship seeds by trying to force their pace of growth and gain a reputation for money-grubbing, asset-sweating callousness. People don't do business long with amateurs or rapacious, self-interested merchants of greed.

The model we subscribe to does have a rational component. And yes, there are sequential steps in the process, which increase the likelihood that the potential client or customer will place their order with you rather than the other person. But the key differentiator that makes the process effective is the sincerity of the operator.

Organisations that don't do new business properly tend to rely on individualistic salespeople who are good at closing, or on massive, cumbersome, machine-like Customer Relationship programmes. They either work on the basis that when the moment comes – when the potential customer is at the point where they want to buy – the sale will go to the salesperson who best closes the deal; or they place all their faith in the impersonal 'machine', believing that if they send enough unsolicited emails, newsletters and thought-leadership papers to new business prospects, and have a high-profile online presence, new clients and new revenues are sure to follow.

These two approaches tend to put a premium either on the 'red-in-tooth-and-claw' sales hounds who are motivated by commission, and who know how to turn up the sales pressure in the last few metres of the process; or on the efficient implementation of an ongoing 'customer outreach programme' by a middle-management minion who is usually disconnected from the main fee earners in the business and who places all her faith in spreadsheets. Chances are that the former will use all manner of tricks and schemes to convert that sale: special offers, discounts, added value packages – anything just to get the sale over the line when the opportunity arises. And the latter will spend their whole self-justifying existence updating new business status reports, doing pipeline analysis reports (showing lots of activity but no tangible results) for the board and creating the appearance of proactive marketing whilst running around busily creating pitch and Request for Information documents for practice leaders who see them as a sort of glorified clerk.

Both approaches are wrong. One is a total lottery run by egotistical chancers (think of door-to-door salespeople, for example); the other is a sort of civil service department, which is normally the first to be axed in an economic downturn because it can never point to any actual value creation over and above the production of a self-perpetuating administrative empire (most professional services organisations we have come across are like this model).

Better salespeople – the diligent farmers – don't rely on being maverick, brilliant gift-of-the-gab merchants or a civil service-style 'Department of Business Development'. Diligent farmers plant their relationship seeds, nurture each contact personally, keep in touch, try to be uniquely useful in each relationship, stay positive and friendly, wait patiently for the right moment in their contact's business cycle and then reap the reward when that person is in the frame to buy. It may take weeks, it may take months, it may even take years. The diligent farmer never loses touch, never gives up, never treats someone as just a number on a revenue forecast report or a ticket to a new Ferrari. Therefore, their new business conversion rates are both higher and more profitable.

The simple secret to their success is that they create a *relationship* with their potential customers that builds cumulatively over time, so that by the time the potential buyer becomes an actual buyer, it is a foregone conclusion that they will buy from the diligent farmer. The diligent farmer already knows everything the potential customer needs and wants. She has been of enormous help giving honest and straightforward counsel over the entire period of the relationship, has learnt all there is to know about this person – their motivations, their requirements, their ambitions, their life story, what and who they hold dear – and has already created a great reputation among the people this potential customer trusts. The diligent farmer has not just *promised* to do certain things that will help, but has actually *done* them, and thus, has proven herself to be trustworthy and reliable. In short, our diligent farmer knows how to act in the best interests of the would-be customer and also make them *feel* that they are acting in their best interests. Contrast this with the commission-remunerated sales-closer who smells blood in the water and circles the would-be customer – with whom they have absolutely no pre-existing relationship – like a predator waiting to notch up another 'kill'. Or the impersonal bureaucrat who treats every prospective client as an income column on a file management system, to be mailed with generic e-spam or invited to the next lacklustre event in the vain belief that they are nurturing close relationships and accelerating them down the new business funnel.

The model we espouse combines the science of systematic, rational process with the art of being likeable and building trust between human beings. You can be systematic and rational without being likeable and you will have a degree of success in new business, but the quality of your relationships will be transactional and therefore vulnerable to a diligent farmer. You can be immensely likeable, but have no method or system and you will bring in a decent amount of new business sporadically. Combine the two, combine the science and the art, and you will be unstoppable. You will have deep, long-lasting, robust relationships with your clients, which are immune from your competitors' advances because they are based on trust and validated by delivery. Very, very few people do both. Why? Because they think it takes too long and we need results *now*. Why do we need results now? Because, more often than not, we turn the new business tap on only when the need for new revenue is *urgent*. Only then do we realise there isn't a sufficient volume of relationships filtering down the funnel to convert enough new business to hit our targets. So we let loose the sales dogs, the predators who can close deals quickly, and we flail about wildly looking for opportunistic scraps to generate income. Meanwhile, the diligent farmer has put their human seed-corn into the top of the hopper and nurtured it through the funnel so that there is a constant stream of potential clients who are not just in the market to buy now, but are predisposed to buy from the diligent farmer – because they've been looked after for the last six months, a year, three years, or even decade.

Just like farming, new business is a long game, not a quick one. So start now, if you haven't already. And never stop. Do it in real life (IRL) and do it virtually, online. Both are tools that help the diligent farmer to farm better. Do this, and you will always have a constant and abundant stream of contacts that will turn into contracts.

Be the diligent farmer, not the sales dog or the spreadsheet bureaucrat. It might be less macho, it might be less glamorous, it might require different skills than keyboard competence, but it will work a lot better, be much less stressful and produce far superior and far more consistent results. It will be easier.

There is another advantage to adopting the diligent farmer model and it's this: no more cold calls. No one likes making cold calls. With this method you never have to make another cold call in your career. Any calls you do make will be warm, because you will use all the media at your disposal to start and nurture the relationship, because every prospect you will ever want is now reachable anywhere in the world and, most importantly of all, because there is so much information about each and every one of them, you will be able to tailor your message so it is highly personalised and relevant to their situation and personality type.

It is now possible to know many thousands of people simultaneously and in relative depth from the information you glean about them online. A diligent farmer knows every member of the herd and understands them. The diligent farmer knows every inch of every acre of the land, because it serves his and his animals' best interests to do so. We discuss how to network and prospect virtually in depth in Chapter 20 (p.235). But, in a nutshell, as the world has moved increasingly online, we believe that whilst the technology offers new and more sophisticated ways to connect, catalyse and nurture relationships, the same fundamental rules apply to how people must engage with one another. We have seen entire businesses thrive online and build communities of new clients and customers where no one has ever met face to face. The interface of a screen is not an inhibitor to catalysing relationships, rather it is an alternative to IRL and a wonderful adjunct. Relationships can be built very effectively online – but, as in real life, if the technology is abused, if the intrusion into people's personal space is overdone, if the approach is too clumsy or inconsiderate, the result will be no sale. In fact, it will be an *anti*-sale, because you will have made an enemy. Diligent farmers are not in the business of making enemies.

CHAPTER 2

A BUSINESS DEVELOPMENT MASTERCLASS

'Are you not entertained? Is this not why you are here?'
Maximus, *Gladiator*

The 18.05 Pullman service to Penzance in Cornwall departs every weekday evening from platform four at London's Paddington Station. It is the last remaining dining car on the British railway system. If you have a reservation, then you have a first-class ticket. But if, like most of us, you are too mean to pay for a first class ticket but want to be fed in convivial company for the marathon journey to the most south-westerly corner of England, then you arrive on the concourse twenty minutes before departure and wait in line chatting to your potential fellow diners hoping for a seat at the table. Once the tables are laid up the staff open the door and invite on board anyone who has a reservation. Then they seat the savvy customers who have waited; there is always space to accommodate the line. The accidental dinner party has begun.

The accidental dinner party is the finest school for business development in the land. It doesn't call itself a school, nor will you get a diploma or any other qualification. But several hours after embarking you will emerge at your destination older, wiser, replete and having experienced a masterclass in the art. Although the whole thing has been so effortlessly enjoyable you won't have noticed that you just sat through a masterclass. It has been fun, interesting, engaging, life-affirming and, as all the best business development is, a game. You will not have noticed, because it has been disguised simply as good conversation.

Once on board, you will be shown to a table either for two people or four people. A table for four is best because then there are three strangers dining with you and not just the one opposite you, as there is on a table for two. If you are on a table for two and your dining companion is a bore, you have a long journey ahead of you. So, you choose a table for four. Seated with you are three other random diners. There is no rhyme or reason to it; it is just first come, first served, and you end up seated with whoever the chief steward has put you next to and opposite. That's the genius of it. So much of our lives we try to control every aspect of who we are with, to choose for ourselves our companions. But the 18.05 takes away that predeterminism along with any element of choice. You should let it. It *needs* to be accidental. It is an *accidental* dinner party. These people are your companions for the duration of the trip.

There is one man who we remember above all others. Mike. Remember him, from Chapter 1? He was a regular on this service and although we sat with him only once, we had the joy and privilege to hear him in action from further down the carriage several times. He was a solicitor, a partner at a practice in the City of London. He was semi-retired and he came up to London from his home in Torquay several times a month. He was also a mediator – a qualified intermediary used to solve disputes between warring parties so they didn't go to the trouble and expense of going to court. He was an interesting man. A *bon viveur* and a raconteur. He was also the finest new business developer in the world.

This man was a walking Zen master in how to prospect for new clients. He almost couldn't help himself. So practised was he that it had become part of who he was, it had become second nature to him. The remarkable thing was he never closed a deal or attempted to hustle, he never spouted about what he did or how he could help or bang on that he had this product or that service. He never proffered his business card. But whenever one of his dining companions moved to get their coats and cases from the luggage rack readying to disembark after dinner, without fail, every one of them would ask him for *his* business card, usually with a statement like:

'Thank you so much for a wonderful couple of hours. I've really enjoyed your company. I hope you don't mind me asking, but I would love to get your business card. What we discussed has made me think and I would like to follow up on our conversation. Would that be all right?'

The secret of this man's brilliance was that he never went after his fellow diners for their business. They always chased after him. How did he get them to do that? Simple. He helped them. He put information that was relevant to each of them into their heads and then just left it there. He let them fill in the gap; he let them identify their own needs.

Whoever he was sitting with, he would find out what they did and who they were. It wasn't difficult – all those sharing a table swapped information by way of an introduction at the start of the journey. And wine, shared, did the rest. But this man really listened. And over the course of the dinner – usually it lasts at least a couple of hours or more – he would share a little of himself and how he spent his time and maybe tell the odd funny or interesting story, but then he would listen to everyone else and what they did. And for each person he would casually mention that there was a piece of legislation or a new White Paper going through the EU or Parliament which might have some repercussions for that person's business. It might be worth their while to look it up and just check it out. That was it. Then he would return to the general conversation or tell another story. Without exception they would all get off and want to follow up the conversation with him. He had piqued their curiosity by posing them a potential problem and, by implication, positioned himself as a potential provider of a solution. But it was all implied and never stated. It didn't need to be explicit.

If you pick apart the elements that make this an exemplary story of sales technique or of how to network or of how to prospect for new business, they are phenomenally simple. But for all their simplicity, they were born out of massive experience, an innate grasp of human nature, a supreme command of his field of competence (the law and how it was applied to numerous industries) and a love of company. We don't think he was cynical. We do think he shared his knowledge and expertise out of a genuine desire to be of service. But his generosity repaid him generously – every time.

He understood the maxim: if you wish to prosper, first learn to please.

Isn't it much cleverer to get people queuing to buy what you've got than trying to get them to see the world your way and bend them to your will? Isn't it easier to get people to come to you and not the other way around? Isn't it sensible to give them enough to make them want more? Most people don't do this; instead, they overwhelm the person they are 'targeting' with too much information in order to get them to see they know everything there is to know about their specialism. The result is predictable – the target is repelled rather than attracted. Pushiness has its place. But in the game of seduction, nonchalance (not being too keen) works best. Ask any Casanova. Make them want more. Hold back. Give enough to pique their interest and wait for them to come calling.

'But I have targets,' we hear you say. 'I have to be proactive. I can't just sit around and wait for new business to come to me.'

No, you can't. Which is why we are not advocating you just sit around and wait. The reason you suddenly need lots of new business is that your company hasn't been actively creating contacts which can turn into contracts for way too long. Just because you have an urgent need for new business now doesn't mean the potential clients out there share your urgency.

Yes, you do need to go out and generate business. But in the early stages it serves better to approach gently, by first establishing or re-establishing contact, with enquiry about possible issues they are facing, expressing interest and a genuine will to help. Focus on establishing contact, on getting them to register your existence in a positive way. Focus on letting them know you're there. If you rush to close, you will screw it up and be back at square one again. If you try to meet, greet, sell, close and notch up a sale all in one hit, you're in a short-term numbers game and your potential clients will see you coming as the avaricious, self-centred short-termist that you are. And if you are in a short-term numbers game, you won't have much success or fun, you won't make lasting relationships and you'll burn out real quick. Why do you think the staff turnover in cold-calling telesales operations is so high? Answer: because, if it is not trained properly, it is a joyless, soul-destroying job which kills your spirit and adds nothing to the sum of human kindness – and which has a minute sales strike rate. Our way is much more lucrative and much more fun. Trust us.

At this stage of the process you are a fisher of people – like our friend on the 18.05 to Penzance from Paddington. Slowly, slowly, catchy fishy. The trick is to get enough nets out in the water that you always have a catch about to land. Do this, and you will never go hungry.

CHAPTER 3

SHOW UP . . . AND KEEP ON SHOWING UP

'80 per cent of success is showing up'
Woody Allen

Woody Allen, the New York-based film director and actor, famously said that '80 per cent of success is showing up.' Whatever you think of him, this insight is still true.

The only guarantee is that if you *don't* show up, nothing will happen – or, at least, nothing different from the everyday norm. Think back through life to all those occasions when you didn't want to go to this party or bother with attending that function. And then think of the opportunities that came from being at that event – sometimes the most unexpectedly wonderful things happen to us when we just make the effort to show up. We meet our future life partner. We make a lifelong friendship. We make a contact who becomes a client for a decade. We meet someone who offers us a job. Stuff happens when you show up. Amazing stuff.

When you show up, anything can happen. Creating that possibility is one of the secrets to winning new business. Most people don't get this. They think that new business is entirely deliberate, planned, systematic, with little or no room for random coincidence. They think that new business is akin to a train journey – it has a final destination (winning the contract) and certain pre-scheduled stops along the line on the way to the final destination: prospecting activity such as a letter or an offer of a seminar or an invitation to a meeting, a request for information, a request for proposal, a formal pitch – then a win! These people are wrong. They slave over spreadsheets and databases of contacts and try to bring some order to the chaotic art of human relationship building. They see it as a linear process.

Now, there is room for order in new business and there is room for science. But new business starts with randomness. You are not on a train (well, unless you are actually on the 18.05); you are an atom whizzing around the new business universe looking to bump into other atoms.

Most of us travel through life – and, by extension, through our business life – in quite an ordered way. We seek to impose structure and predictability on our personal universe. We gravitate to the familiar and the similar. Therefore, after the initial discomfort of being forced into random situations early in life – such as moving to a new school, college or university, where we are forced to meet loads of strangers – we seek to maximise control over the people who circle our lives.

We spend as much time as possible in the company of people who are just like us. We like people who look like us, share our values, see the world the same way, share our interests, talk like us, value the same things as we do. Sometimes, we even share the same hairstyle and mode of dress. Don't believe us? Check out the person you've agreed to have lunch with today, or the person you're travelling with whilst you read this book. Or the people you're on your way to meet. Or the friends you have on Instagram or Facebook. Birds of a feather . . . you know the rest.

It's the same when we go to a work event or an industry dinner or a conference. We seek out the familiar faces. The known quantities – the people just like us (usually our colleagues) and we stick to them like glue. That way we don't have to make the effort to meet new people. That way we won't run the risk of any awkwardness or running out of conversation or of having to bust in on a group of strangers who are talking fascinatedly to one another.

By behaving like this we are effectively – if not consciously – eradicating the very things which make life more interesting and new business success infinitely more attainable: serendipity. Randomness. Haphazardness. Chance. Next time you are at an event, when it's time for the coffee break, be brave: seek out the person who looks least like you, who you feel you might find irritating. Go up to them and introduce yourself. Miracles can happen if you are open and adventurous.

Everyone has a story about how they met their partner or how they made best friends for life with the random stranger they were roomed with in the first term at college. One client told us how, at the airport, he was made to unpack his suitcase and wear six layers of winter clothing to avoid paying excess baggage on a flight from a thirty-degree Sydney in Australia to a four-degree London. When he got to his seat as the last passenger to board, he started stripping off each layer and stowing them in the overhead locker. He got down to his original skimpy outfit of shorts and a T-shirt.

'Why stop there?' said the woman – a complete stranger – sitting in the seat next to him. They were married the next year.

Our first assignment came from a friend David had first got to know eighteen years earlier, on day one of a new job. He went on to become godfather to one of David's sons and got us our first gig addressing a conference in Siem Reap, Cambodia. It was a contract that evolved into a revenue of over $3 million – useful when you've just started your own business.

What do stories like this tell us? They tell us how life and business *really* work. They tell us that it is the random connections we make in life that normally have the greatest consequences. They tell us that if you open your mouth to start a dialogue with a stranger there is just no telling where it will lead.

Which is why it is so mind-bogglingly strange that most of the time in life and in business, we go all 'methodical' on ourselves and try to *minimise* the number of random interactions we have. We call this 'targeting' and it is the greatest enemy of effective new business development in existence. (There is a place for targeting, but not yet, not at this stage.)

We have a destructive and counterproductive tendency to try to preselect our potential new contacts, in the name of being efficient. In seeking to find even more people 'like us' or people *we* want to talk to (but who may have zero interest in talking to us, a possibility we totally ignore), we reduce down to as near zero as possible the chance of making genuinely random connections. But lest we forget, atoms bumping into each other in seemingly haphazard coincidence is the stuff life is made of. It's called 'Brownian Motion' and it is all around us. A common description of this phenomenon is that in the fluid or flexible state atoms bump into each other and move in random directions. So it is with any *new* human contact – there is nothing fixed in either the relationship or the certainty of one forming. This is the essence of new business development. By contrast, *existing* client relationships are 'solid state' relationships. They are held in position and stable, according to the same principle: in a solid state, atoms are held in position and can only vibrate. In other words, if you regard stable relationships – between you and existing clients – as 'solid', you can see that being held in position and vibrating gently is a good thing. It sounds like an accurate description of a married partnership or an ongoing business partnership. But in the universe outside stable relationships, where you are seeking inherently *un*stable relationships – i.e. potential new relationships which have not yet formed and are therefore in a fluid state – you'd better get used to, and actually use, the fact that randomness is the natural state of play.

> **Stop trying to control your networking universe. It works best when you let it be in its natural state: random.**

Time and again we hear companies saying that they don't want to waste effort and resources chasing and wooing people and clients who will be a waste of time. This attitude exposes a fundamental misunderstanding of (i) *how new business prospecting works;* (ii) *where they are in the process;* and (iii) *a misplaced belief that they can 'turn on the charm' when it is needed.*

(i) It belies a fundamental misunderstanding of how new business works because the game at the outset is to *maximise* opportunity, not to limit it. Everybody thinks that by being targeted they are eliminating wasted effort and being clever with scarce resources. In conventional new business, people focus all their time on those few prospects who might be valuable to them *now*. This is completely the wrong approach. Why? Because targeting in this way excludes future buyers. In his article 'Quantum marketing', Peter Weinberg of LinkedIn demonstrates the importance of spreading your net as wide as possible for new business: '. . . every four years, around 40 per cent of our members change their industry, seniority, function, company size, and company'. People move on and move up. If you focus only on those who are useful right now, you will always be in the business of ambulance chasing. You will never get ahead and develop a robust pipeline with prospects trickling down it for evermore.

Here is yet more proof:

If we take the example of evolutionary biology, the two evolutionary 'strategies' are termed r-selection, for those species that produce many 'cheap' offspring and live in *unstable* environments; and K-selection, for those species that produce few 'expensive' offspring and live in *stable* environments. As we have seen from the Brownian Motion analogy, not only is the natural state of new business unstable, but the economic environment post-COVID-19 is the most unstable business environment we have experienced since the Second World War. We are working within a doubly unstable environment. It therefore suits our networking needs to adopt the r-selection strategy: to get as many conversations and random interactions out there as possible in order to maximise the chances of at least some of them turning to gold. Focused attention directed narrowly at a few, highly targeted opportunities is the appropriate strategy for stable environments. For existing clients. In times of uncertainty, the r-selection strategy pays off best. Ask any virus.

(ii) It demonstrates a fundamental misunderstanding of where they are in the process because there is so much more information that needs to be understood and so many more connections that might emanate from this initial random contact that to close down avenues at this stage is way too early and actually means closing off the possibilities of massive opportunity. Secondarily, by refining your targeting at this stage you may miss the random elephant that wanders into view by focusing exclusively on the stag that you set out to hunt. It's well documented that Viagra wasn't invented as a cure for male erectile disfunction but was originally intended to ease high blood pressure and alleviate chest pain due to heart disease. As with drug efficacy so with relationship efficacy: be open to, not blinkered by, potential significance. If judged as a cure for high blood pressure and chest pain, Viagra was a failure. Yet it is one of the most famous drugs in the world and beloved of many. Let the

Law of Unintended Consequences play its role in your new business efforts.

(iii) Too many people think that they will be incredibly persuasive, charming, skilful in conversation and dazzling when they need to be, as if they can turn it on like a light switch. Most people can't do that – they need to practise. As much as possible. If the only time you turn on the sales charm is when it *really* matters, you will, likely as not, crash and burn. Because you are out of practice. Like any skill, the more you practise it, the luckier you get.

Success can come in disguise

Therefore, if you are invited to something – or even if you are not – show up. You never know what might happen. One thing is for sure – if you don't show up, absolutely nothing will happen, guaranteed. Turning up starts possibilities.

Then it's up to you to keep going.

New business is a game of chase. It takes tenacity and focus and you must never, never, never, never, ever give up.

Keep showing up

It's not enough just to show up. You have to keep showing up.

80 per cent of sales require five follow-up calls after the meeting. 44 per cent of sales representatives give up after one follow-up.

We all know that persistence pays. Sometimes, just to be the last one standing is enough to win the prize. Yet few people

* Aja Frost, '60 Key Sales Statistics That'll Help You Sell Smarter in 2021', Hubspot, blog.hubspot.com/sales/sales-statistics

demonstrate the tenacity and perseverance necessary to succeed, or the foresight to start now in order to reap the harvest in the future rather than immediately (which they expect to do). People want instant results. They want to turn up and walk away with first prize with no real preparation made or time expended. Life does not work that way.

Most people – even those whose job it is to be persistent sales-people – fall at the first hurdle. And if they don't fall at the first hurdle, they fall at the second or the third. Or the fourth hurdle.

When David worked for a top advertising agency in London, his number-one new business 'target' was a certain well-known fast food restaurant chain. The marketing director was a lovely guy, with a great reputation in the industry. David and his boss stayed in touch with him regularly. Very regularly. Very, very regularly. He must have thought they were stalkers. They invited him to the tennis at Wimbledon, they made presentations when they had secretly filmed the counter service experience at various of his restaurants and his competitors' restaurants. They bombarded him with strategy papers, research surveys, brand audits and films of families interacting with each other in front of the TV (way before *Gogglebox*) – *anything* to keep dialogue going and, hopefully, relevant. This went on for years. Four years to be precise. David rang up frequently and never got put through – the marketing director was always in a meeting or out of the office or away somewhere 'but I'll let him know you called', said his personal assistant. Then, one day, out of the blue and just when he was expecting the usual Friday afternoon polite-but-firm brush-off, the PA piped: 'Oh, I'm glad you called. He wants to talk to you about something. I'll just put you through.'

Blow me down. David cleared his throat and sat up straight.

'Hello, David. I'm glad you've called. Look, we've been noticing that there seems to be something quite big going on in the coffee world [Starbucks was sweeping all before it in the UK and the rest of the world] and we've been asked by our global team to pilot something new here in the UK.'

He went on to explain that the restaurant chain had recently bought a small independent coffee chain in the UK in order to have a chance to experiment in the new and rapidly growing area of coffee shops. The marketing director knew that David's agency were no slouches at strategy and research, and invited them to come down from London to a UK Executive Committee meeting near Bath to give a view of how best to take advantage of the opportunity.

Could they attend? Yes, they could. And they did. And they sufficiently impressed the UK Executive Committee to win an assignment to run all the positioning, packaging and in-store design and advertising for this new venture.

OK. It wasn't the core restaurant advertising account. But it was a way in – a chance to shine. It was a foot in the door with the whole organisation.

Moral: If you keep saying 'we're here' and keep trying to be useful, you have an outside chance that one day, when you knock on the door, it will actually open. And once it's open, you're in.

Say 'YES'

Challenge yourself to say 'yes' to every invitation you get in a month or three months and force yourself to go. You know what your mother used to say when you didn't want to go to school: 'You'll enjoy it when you get there,' and she was right.

Go to interesting events where you could potentially meet like-minded people and even prospective clients. Great places for these are:

- Private members' clubs. They often have events that are open to the public for a small fee (or you could join the club if it looks like its members are interesting);

- How To Academy events;
- Speakers bureau events. They often showcase their speakers to potential corporate buyers, usually senior decision-makers;
- Media owner masterclasses;
- Trade- or industry-specific events such as the Marketing or Law Societies;
- Accept any invitation to a special event you wouldn't normally get to attend.

Many of these events are online. Ways to get noticed are to submit questions for the speaker in advance, be a speaker yourself (and watch the world come to you), and to socialise the event on LinkedIn in order to be useful and to generate dialogue, discussion and make people aware who may not have been able to attend.

Top tips for your next event where you don't know anyone:

- Don't wait until you are desperate (you're down to your last client; you've lost your job) to start networking; create relationships and contacts throughout your career.
- Know why you're going to an event – what are you looking for? To learn something new? Find out who's on the panel and the guest list.
- Have some business cards to hand. Yes, they are as cutting edge as the fax machine but it's still a quicker way of passing on your details. In Asia, they are a ritual to help the business of doing business along.
- Circulate. This is for your benefit as well as everyone else's. It's tempting when you find someone that you get on well with to monopolise them for the whole evening. Try not to. Mingle and move on. Unless you really fancy them, of course, in which case monopolise away – how refreshing to meet someone IRL rather than online.

- Follow up. So much of business development is about following up – saying thank you, keeping in contact, inviting them to something you think they would be interested in, etc. But so many people don't bother and if you do, you stand out.
- If someone helps you, help someone else. It's good karma and what we call 'psychological income'.

Keep in mind, as an anonymous quote from the internet once said, 'Networking is about listening with the aim of advancing someone else's agenda, not your own.'

CHAPTER 4

SUMMARY AND WHAT TO EXPECT FROM PART II

Business development is all about catalysing relationships: creating connections between human beings that cause transformational change.

Our job as a catalyst is to be the person whose talk, enthusiasm or energy causes others to be more friendly, enthusiastic or energetic in response. But our amazing personality can only get us so far. If we want to turn a contact into a contract, we need to be highly tuned in to the subtleties of what is being said or implied.

Our partner, who was a great listener and very good at reading between the lines, attended a conference in Istanbul where the CEO of Unilever had been invited to speak for forty minutes to an audience of marketers and agency executives. At the end of the forty minutes, our partner had spotted seventeen 'briefs' in the speech – seventeen issues that he had identified as areas where the CEO needed help. Because the rest of the audience was asleep through the speech, they had all missed them. This was a conference for which people had flown in from all over the world to stay for three days and nights, accommodated in lavish hotel rooms; wined, dined and entertained on the Bosporus, at huge expense; and where the main topic of focus was – you guessed it – how to win new business. Our partner pointed out the seventeen opportunities that the client had 'dropped' into his speech to our host's CEO, and, luckily, this man was no slouch. So he set to engaging with the Unilever client over dinner that night to probe in more detail how he and his team could be of assistance. But if we hadn't been there, millions of dollars would have gone elsewhere.

Being alert to the opportunity when it eventually comes is critical. If you miss that opportunity and let it slip by, unnoticed, then you have failed in new business.

The best catalysts have their 'radar' switched on

When you are in new business mode, you must be switched 'on'. This is not a passive pursuit. You must be alive to any and all opportunities. This is something we learned primarily by studying negotiation technique. In negotiations, the use of language is vitally important. Trained negotiators hate negotiating with untrained negotiators because they so often fail to pick up on the subtleties and signals that are constantly being dropped into the dialogue to move things along. When you are negotiating, there is a world of difference between the response 'I understand' and 'I agree'. An untrained ear doesn't hear this difference and it often causes huge problems down the road when one party says they only said they 'understood' what the other person said, whereas the other party thought they had agreed to that point.

A large part of the work we do with people to help them become better at securing new business is to switch on their internal radar. We all have radar. Normally, we associate it with airports and aeroplanes, but people have radar too. The trouble is, 99 per cent of the time it's switched off.

When you meet new people, either in a social or a work situation, we are normally 'on' for the beginning of the interaction.

Then we stop paying attention. And once we're 'off', all that lovely, useful information that is being thrown our way by the people we are talking with is missed. Switching on your radar is about using all your senses, plus your common sense, to collect all the information you receive from people, consciously. It must always be switched on.

When you meet new people – or, indeed, any people – your senses are capable of picking up the most extraordinary amount of information every second. How they stand or sit, their posture: is it aggressive, defensive or neutral? Their demeanour: is it up, down, distracted, moody, alert, amused? What are they are wearing? How do they look? Where is their attention focused? How does their voice sound? Do they make too little or too much eye contact? Do they use language in a short, clipped manner, or are they expansive and verbose? These questions may seem difficult to answer but your senses are finely tuned to pick up on these cues. Normally, we just focus on what they are saying (at least for a little while). We miss so much more by not paying attention to everything else.

If your radar is always fully on, you will have a much richer picture of the person or people you are with and you will pick up so much more information that might be useful either now or in the future. Oh, and because most of us aren't superhuman, write everything you learn down as soon as you can so you don't forget it.

Be open to the random, to chance and serendipity

Following the release of a new book on business called *On Purpose*, we had just delivered the speech that accompanied the book to a group of members at the Chartered Institute of Marketing in a cold school hall in the East End of London. At the end of the talk, a woman approached us to say how much she had enjoyed it, that she knew 'the Alan Sugar of Barbados' and that she was determined we must work for him. Over the next few weeks this woman kept getting in touch to organise a follow-up meeting. She then insisted we create a proposal to brand a luxury property development in the Caribbean, and asked for a set of our credentials to pass on to this mythical, Sugar-like figure, whom she represented. To be frank, it all sounded a little far-fetched – too good to be true. We were a tad dubious but we humoured her and played along. Weren't we nice?

Well, talk about looking a gift horse in the mouth. She phoned us in June (the speech had been made in February, so you see why we might have been a bit sceptical) to say that her contact had been very impressed and wanted to meet us in London. She divulged the name of this mythical potential benefactor and one Google search later we were all ears. And so began our Bajan adventure. The project ran for six months and netted us more than $1 million plus several weeks in the Caribbean swimming with turtles.

Don't close down opportunities too soon. Remember, new business is an unstable environment which needs a suitable evolutionary strategy; cast your net as wide as possible. Never close a door on someone who wants to work with you, however far-fetched the opportunity may seem. You just never know where it might lead. Hopefully, to a beach in the tropics.

Show up. And keep showing up

In the depths of COVID-19 lockdown, many of us looked back with rueful incredulity, thinking of all those events we failed to turn up to because, despite accepting the invitation months ago, on the day itself we 'didn't feel like it'. At the point when the weekly trip to Tesco was the nearest we got to social interaction, we made desperate promises to ourselves. Never again would we face the prospect of attending a talk or a panel interview or – heaven – an agency party and consider not turning up because we'd rather be at home. We've spent a long time at home. Now is the time to get out there and get meeting people. Be visible. Be helpful. Take advantage of people's enthusiasm and energy for events that previously would have had high dropout rates. We predict that the novelty of crowds will take a long time to wear off once social distancing restrictions finally come to an end.

Talk to strangers – there's no telling where it will lead

Lest we give you the impression that we are two Pollyanna-ish characters, hopping and skipping through life with never a cross word and always with a smile on our faces, we can confirm that we too are human. We have moods. Sometimes we are grumpy. Sometimes we don't feel like talking. However, we have learned over the years that the energy you give out is the energy you get back. Louisa used to cringe when her in-laws came up from Devon and started talking to people on the Tube. NO ONE DOES THAT IN LONDON. And yet, guess what? When her parents-in-law started making conversation, complete strangers – not all of them tourists – chatted back and, in those moments, they made connections which enhanced their whole experience of the trip.

Similarly, we were once on a flight to Geneva and sat in between rows of people on either side of the aisle, ahead of us and behind us, who were all from the same company and on a jolly to a ski resort. As you can imagine, spirits were high. But not with us. We were on our way to a work meeting and were getting a bit po-faced about the noise around us. After a bit of huffing and puffing, we thought, *Sod it!*, and started chatting to the people next to us to find out where they were going and why.

By the end of the flight we'd got an invitation to their aprés-ski party which sadly, due to the fact we were a) working and b) middle-aged, we had to decline. But, 'leaning in' and chatting instead of sitting rigidly trying to pretend a rave is not happening in the seats around us did make the flight more interesting.

Finally, remember that every friend, boyfriend, girlfriend, husband, wife, colleague or client was once a stranger to you. Make the effort! Be pleasant! You never know where it might lead.

Be a diligent farmer with your network

Building your network takes an investment of care, time and attention but will pay off in the end. Work consistently, shepherd your flock and shield it from danger. A diligent farmer's interests are best served by serving others' interests brilliantly. A diligent farmer is not cynical. They will not approach their flock thinking, What can I get from them?, rather their purpose is to try to be uniquely useful in the relationship. Be sincere – nurture each contact personally. This is a marathon not a sprint – never lose touch, never give up. You will reap the reward when the prospect is ready to buy.

It's a game – enjoy it!

The simplest answer to the question, 'Why be a catalyst?', is because it is enjoyable. As we've said before, our job as catalysts is to be the person whose talk, enthusiasm, or energy causes others to be more friendly, enthusiastic or energetic in response. Who wouldn't want to be the person that makes that happen? And, as a catalyst, we are playing a game. The game of new business. This is a game where we make up the rules because there are no rules. Only in new business do you have the power to make money just by being yourself. It's all about chemistry: how your actions can cause a reaction.

What to expect from PART II

In the next section, we turn our focus to you and the prospect. As a catalyst, you're in the business of ensuring your actions create a reaction with the prospect – the chemical reaction that will transform you both.

Understanding what you're dealing with is key. Which is why we've asked a number of clients who have worked with agencies, suppliers and trusted advisors over the years to share some of their perspectives on what works well and to vent about their pet peeves.

Understanding who you're dealing with will give you the edge. The first time you meet a prospect you want to be able to quickly build rapport between you both. Having the ability to spot, at pace, what type of person you might be dealing with helps speed up that rapport. We'll explain how you do it.

Part II is all about chemistry – that complex emotional or psychological interaction between people. It's intangible, exciting, often difficult to explain but instantly recognisable when it happens. What are you waiting for? Let's begin.

CHEMISTRY: ACTION AND REACTION

PART II

CHEMISTRY: ACTION
AND REACTION

CHAPTER 5

HOW DO YOU MAKE THEM FEEL?

'Some cause happiness wherever they
go; others whenever they go'
Oscar Wilde

'But what will I *say* when I meet Pardeep?' whined the managing director of the media agency, when he got an appointment to meet the new marketing director at the company his agency was pitching to.

'Your job is not to say anything, but to listen,' we replied, earning his enmity from the beginning. This was our first exposure to the pitch team the managing director was leading for the most valuable pitch in the media marketplace of that decade. But we persisted – that is our lot as new business experts, trying to get our clients to behave in a way that will result in a win rather than in the way most organisations behave when left to their own devices, which is to do everything they can do to *prevent* a win.

Too many people – including this managing director – mistake talking for being fascinating. They mistake droning on endlessly about themselves or about what is unique about their product or service (it really isn't unique, sorry to break it to you) for creating rapport with the client.

If you make people *feel listened to and heard* they will

remember you. Why? Because so few people make others feel that way. Instead, people talk and talk and talk endlessly about themselves. They crash on about their own opinions or experiences. Everything you say reminds them of something they once did or thought, and everywhere you have travelled reminds them of their own anecdote about that place (which, naturally, they visited before you and more stylishly). They interrupt you and monopolise the conversation. This behaviour does not impress or make friends; it simply creates resentment..

In ordinary business, people tend to have prepared something they want to say, or, more usually, when they are meeting a new business prospect for the first time, they have prepared a list of clever-sounding questions to ask. They become so wedded to their questions and to glancing down to see what question they need to ask next, that they stop listening to the other person's answers and lose the thread of what is being spoken about. By focusing on the list of questions and not on building the relationship with the person they are talking to, they break rapport and the interview becomes a mission to get through all the questions rather than to really understand what makes this person tick.

Experienced TV, radio and podcast interviewers show us how it should be done. The really good ones share a secret: in advance of the interview they think very hard about the questions they want to ask the person they are interviewing. They commit them to memory or put a one-word prompt for each question on an index card and place it in their pocket just as they go 'live'. That way, they free themselves up to focus entirely on the interviewee. By doing so, they can pick up not just *what* is being said but also *how* it is being said. They can be sensitive to mood, tone, body language. They can sense discomfort or someone warming to a theme. Free from the tyranny of a written list of questions to get through, they create genuine rapport with their subject. Because they know the questions they might want to ask, they are free to let the conversation roam into areas where the interviewee might divulge more about themselves or their needs than they would otherwise have done if they stuck to the original list of questions.

This is called 'being present'. Whole libraries of books have been written about this subject and its companion, mindfulness. In spite of someone's capacity to meditate or be in the moment in their yoga class or at home, it all just goes out of the window for most people in the heat of a new business meeting. We are so self-conscious and egocentric, so busy trying to impress the new business prospect with our genius and knowledge that we forget to focus on the one thing we should focus on: them.

The job is not to worry about what you will say. The job is to get the other person saying things.

Remember: everyone has a story. Make it your mission to find out what that story is. If you do find out, not only will you discover that the person you are meeting is genuinely fascinating, they will also think you are fabulous.

The job is to send the other person away with the strong feeling that (a) they have been heard; (b) that they have enjoyed their time with you; and (c) that you have their best interests at heart.

How not to network

When you meet someone new – whether business or personal – they will pick up on your vibe. They will respond to your energy. They will react to the aura you create. But beware. There are some among us who think they are being lively and amusing and charming but are actually having the exact reverse effect. These are the serial networkers – those who have made a professional living out of collecting thousands of 'very close, personal friends'. They are the ones who have become blinded to their own counterproductive habits. They are the ones who, in thinking they exude charm, actually end up being oleaginous – oily, insincere and not to be trusted. They think of themselves as 'charmers'. They network because they want something – your scalp. They want your scalp for their trophy collection, for their little black book.

How do you spot one of these people and how do you avoid becoming one? First of all, how do you spot one? Here's an easy acronym: we call them ANTHONYs:

All about me
Not interested in you
That reminds me of something I did that is a lot more interesting than what you did
Happy to talk over you
Over your shoulder is someone far more useful to me (their eyes constantly scan the room looking for anyone more important)
Never follow up or say thank you if you help them
You are now, apparently, one of five hundred of their closest friends

Secondly, how do you avoid becoming one of these people? Well, you don't *have* to – their strategy does work in some respects. They tend to be laughed at behind their back and they never know if the people they count among their close, personal friends are as manipulative as they are, but they do usually end up with a formidable network of contacts and they are usually very adept at working their network to advantage. The only problem is that it is a transparently transactional relationship, albeit dressed up as a deep and meaningful, mutually respectful and caring one. If you are happy to operate in this way and with the requisite level of Hollywood-esque shallowness, good for you. But it is not for everyone and it is not for us. Why? Because usually these people get seen for what they are: false, self-aggrandising, pompous and out purely for themselves.

Our preferred *modus operandi* is to be sincere – not worthy or moralising – just straight and open and generous without expectation of repayment. We have sound commercial reasons to believe that sincerity pays. It is the same ironic paradox that dictates the rules of dating. Those who glue on a persona in order to be more attractive – especially one that is not true to who they really are – may have some success initially, but it will be short-lived and eventually they will be found out for who they truly are. That does not mean that we do not need to present our most attractive self to the world, but it does mean that if you are too chameleon-like, you will end up living a lie and inhabiting a self that does not feel very comfortable. Fakes are always spotted eventually.

The problem with being a fake, with being an ANTHONY, is that your nakedly selfish agenda gets exposed, and people who spot you might not always give away that they have seen you for what you are. Instead they carry on behaving in a seemingly complicit and cooperative way whilst actually undermining you in the background. We had an associate who only ever got in touch when he wanted a favour. He was called Adam. He did it once too often with us but we played along. He was moving to Asia (because he had alienated most of the Western world, by then, in his chosen sphere of work) to start anew, and he knew that we knew one particular person he wanted to meet. The person he was targeting was the boss of the Asia region in the company where Adam wanted to work. He asked us to set up the meeting. We did. But we briefed the boss to stand him up, which is what he did. We never heard from the associate again – which is what we wanted. Mission accomplished.

Petty? Mean? Not at all. He was a pest. He only ever acted out of his own selfishness and never gave anything to anyone else.

He is a sober reminder to us all that the way we behave usually comes back to haunt us, even if we have no idea who the payback emanated from when it eventually comes. Don't be an Adam because you will be seen for what you are: nakedly ambitious but uncaring about anyone else. Revenge will be meted out to you for your selfishness. Other people are not just passive players in your drama; they are thinking, feeling beings and you cannot treat them as mere pawns in your grand game of life-chess.

Treating people as pawns is the classic mistake that ANTHONYs and Adams make all the time. We can be so full of ourselves that we forget other people are the key players on the stage of their own lives – they are not means to your end, pawns, conduits or playthings.

We all know that you should treat others as you would wish others to treat you. It is an oft-repeated truism that you do not treat anyone, however 'lowly' you might think they are, with discourtesy. You would assume no one still does it. Unfortunately, they do. When people are supposedly on their best behaviour but want to ensure they impress the *right* person, they often focus on impressing *only* that person. Everyone else they treat as subservient. The receptionist, the waiter serving their food, the junior people in the elevator, the cleaners. These people are treated as secondary – people getting in the way of the conversation they want to have with the VIP. But the VIP often notices how you treat other people around them. When it recruits its top executives, Southwest Airlines usually takes a candidate to a restaurant specifically to see how the interviewee treats the restaurant staff – that is literally the only point of the meeting. What's more, the other people – the non-VIPs – either have a veto or are asked for their opinion about the person concerned. For example, a top director from a major organisation wanted to work for Google. As you might imagine, he was a bit full of himself, and with some justification as he had built an awesome reputation during his career. After his first interview he was rejected, and his candidacy didn't proceed any further. He was incensed. He had assumed the first interview was a mere formality with a junior functionary, so he was dismissive of her and her questions – saving himself for someone further up the hierarchy who actually mattered. Oh dear.

'She was just the bloody recruiter!' he complained to us.

QED.

Don't stand on your dignity. Instead, be as humble as the dust. Don't show off, don't brag, don't monopolise the conversation, don't scan the room for someone more important, don't be a bore, don't be 'the big I am'. When we stand on our dignity, it's easy to trip up.

CHAPTER 6

THE CLIENT PERSPECTIVE

'Integrity is doing the right thing, even
when no one is looking'
C. S. Lewis

To help you avoid the pitfalls so many new business practitioners fall into initially, we interviewed a cross section of very senior
and experienced clients for their views of what to do and what
not to do if you are trying to get into dialogue with them. These
clients are all either board-level directors in publicly quoted
companies or have been so. They have all operated at the very top
of big international organisations in fields as diverse as the automotive industry, banking – commercial, investment and retail –
fashion, packaged goods, luxury brands, technology, sport and
telecoms. Between them, the brands they have represented at
the highest level include Giorgio Armani, Barclays Bank, Coca-
Cola, Farfetch, Helmut Lang, Nissan, Royal Bank of Scotland,
Vodafone and Volkswagen. They have been responsible for
buying professional advisory services and, in several cases, have
been on both sides of the fence – as clients but also as sellers of
professional advisory services in various guises.

What they have to say is based on vast experience and is,
therefore, worth heeding if you seek to steal a march on your
competitors.

For the sake of brevity, we have categorised the advice into five major themes, all of which are illustrated with stories and examples of when these clients feel people have got their approach right, and, correspondingly, tales of when people have got their approach woefully wrong.

1. 'Don't call me Dave' – do your research

We have at our disposal the vast weaponry of technology, which allows us to personalise every piece of communication and tailor every approach to a new business prospect. It also enables us to research people and companies more forensically than ever before. We have access to databases, Google and other search engines, and a host of social media – LinkedIn, Facebook, Instagram, Twitter, etc. So there is no excuse for making anything other than a tailored approach to your client prospect. A few minutes carefully invested in these powerful tools will give you chapter and verse on the person whose attention you want to engage. Don't just read what they say about themselves and their career chronology; take note of the way they write, what photo and background they use on their profile, the groups they follow, and read any comments they make about other people or subjects they are interested in. If your radar is on, you will find a wealth of information that should inform the way you engage with them.

And yet. The former chief marketing officer at RBS in the UK complains that of the 10,000 or so speculative emails he has received over his tenure in the role, only a handful – he says just two – have made a genuinely thoughtful, highly personalised approach. The rest have been generic, inappropriately pitched and even annoying.

'I hate being addressed as "Dave". My name is David,' he complains.

'In an attempt to be familiar on email ('Hey Dave . . .') and sound pally, as if they know me, people follow up with a sort of attempt to flatter. For example: "Great what you're doing at the bank," they say – a vague platitude which would be unlikely to have anything behind it, no real understanding of what is actually being done and which would collapse under the most basic questioning. I wish people would stop being superficial and just be human. And then they compound it by trying to get me interested in some proprietary new global tool they have. We're a domestic bank. We aren't really in the market for global tools. It shows a basic lack of understanding – within three sentences – of who I am, how I operate or what my company does. Result: delete.'

David concludes: 'Business is people-to-people. It can be aided by technology, but technology does not obviate the need to understand people. There is a basic lack of homework [being done], a basic lack of preparation.'

This sentiment is echoed by all the clients we spoke with, and is normally the first thing they mention when asked the question: 'What works when people try to connect with you and what doesn't work?'

Giorgio, who has built a highly successful career in the fashion industry, and who has sold into the most famous high-fashion brands in the world, places the need to understand your audience above all other things:

The luxury market is about trust, protecting the relationship. It is not always just about growth. I have friends in every brand, and I understand their language.

This industry works in seasons not in days. Brands change fortunes every season. You have to work on the industry's rhythm – timing is key. If you miss a season, then nothing will happen for at least another three to six months.

In other words, you need to engage with people not just on a human level but also at the appropriate time in their calendar (not in yours), thereby signalling that you understand their industry and have gone to the bother of researching and finding out the particular issues in their world. So many people prospect from the perspective of *their own* needs and calendar. If you do, you will fall at the first fence.

Simon, who works in the automotive industry, agrees and thinks that so many prospectors go badly wrong when they don't get what's on the mind of the person that's in front of them:

> People are asking for my time – the one thing I don't have a lot of – as if that's nothing for me to grant to them. Recognise and acknowledge that I could have been doing something else. And if I grant an hour to you, I will be home an hour later this evening. If you talk to me about stuff that isn't relevant to me right now, you're not actually helping me; you are actually adding to my problems! Instead, talk about what you know is front of mind for me, and tailor your approach to show me how you can help me. Before you come and see me, identify the prevailing challenges and interests I will have [on my radar]. Have a solution to a high-priority challenge you know we are facing. If you come along as, say, a change management consultancy, and you start going on about how you've worked for IBM and GE, even God, and you want to tell me about the process re-engineering work you did for all of them, but meanwhile I'm in the middle of a financial crisis, you are irrelevant. I don't need process re-engineering. Not right now. I have other more pressing stuff I need to focus on.

Research the person, research the industry, and research the company. In the data and information age, there is absolutely no excuse for having to make a cold approach. There is so much information out there to help you create an accurate understanding of the person you want to get to know. There are so many cross references to be pursued – the person's profile on LinkedIn, what people say about them, their résumé of past roles, their extra-curricular activities, the people who know them, who you might know, who can be approached to ask for an introduction to this person. And you can cross-reference with any news about the person or the articles they have written or been quoted in, and ask for a pen portrait of this person from your mutual connection. You are looking for clues as to this person's personality, the tone of voice they use to describe themselves, what they are inter-ested in and commentating about. It is astounding how easy it is to sound well read and clued up if you invest a little time getting to understand and think about the person you want to engage. It is easy to sound impressively well versed in some of the issues they might be tackling just by reading the company annual report, the quarterly results, recent press interviews and the analysts' reports. It is easy to be up-to-date and form a view.

Ask yourself:

- What do you know about the prospect client's business? Not just their marketing or accountancy or law issue but their *overall* business. What did it say in the annual report? What do investors say about it? What is reported in the media? What were the last quarter's results like? What is the forecast? What issues are they dealing with now in the fields of legislation, politics, economics, environmental, demographic, logistics, distribution, consumer and competition?
- What problems can you help them solve?

- Can you help them make a gain or avoid a loss? Can you do it faster, more efficiently, more cost-effectively?
- What's your USP (unique selling proposition)?
- How can you demonstrate the difference you can make for them?
- What's the cost of them doing nothing about the issue you have identified?

2. The kindness of strangers –
connect as people, not prospects

When we seek to do business, something seems to happen in our heads which stops us behaving like normal human beings and starts us behaving like selfish, money-motivated idiots. In our rush to impress, in our hurry to use the begged, borrowed or stolen time we have managed to get with the person we are chasing, we cram in all the impressive things about us and our company at machine-gun speed and hope that something strikes a chord that will then lead on to business.

It won't.

If you regard getting the appointment as the key mission, you are missing the point. If you think that the mission is simply to get face time in front of your new business prospect, or keep them on the phone for as long as possible, then you are in the wrong business. You are not in the business of effective new business acquisition. You are in the business of time-wasting.

This is a long game. It is not a short game. If you try to get the meeting at all costs, you have missed the point. If you truly believe you are *so* persuasive that all it will take for you to convince them of your genius and their immediate need for your service or product is for you to get in front of the prospect, then you are deluded.

We see people use all sorts of ruses to try to create the meeting opportunity. Quite often, people will try to go over the head of the person they want to meet to try to get their boss to force a meeting. Brilliant. How would you react if your boss instructed you to meet someone because your boss knows this person, and says she feels it would be politic for you to meet with them? Would you sit there all ears, hanging on their every word? No. You would do what any red-blooded human being would do – you would acquiesce, put the meeting in your diary, sit there stony-faced, not ask any questions and allocate them exactly the amount of time in the meeting that you have been instructed to give them. Your mindset might be, to put it mildly, hostile.

Simon says he was often being forced into meeting various self-important companies that had relationships higher up the organisation and used them to get in front of him. They never got any business. Their tactic of forcing the meeting was entirely counterproductive.

Getting the meeting isn't the point. Getting the meeting at the right time, on the relevant subject (relevant to the client) and, preferably, teed up by a person whose judgement is trusted by the client, is the goal. Simon contends that if a trusted lieutenant in his team – one of his key direct reports – recommended he talk with this individual or that company, and the topic had a bearing on a specific challenge he was facing at the time, or if someone in business whose judgement he respected suggested he meet with a particular company, then that was an entirely different matter.

If it's proving difficult to see the person you want to see, work out who are the members of the team *surrounding* that person who have his ear. If the invitation to meet is issued through a trusted mouth into the prospect's ear, and comes as a recommendation, then not only will you get the meeting but you will also get the meeting with the prospect client who is in the right mindset – who wants to hear what you have to say. And remember, if it works out and turns into an engagement, the recommendation also helps to burnish the reputation of the trusted lieutenant with her or his boss.

We won an important contract with Nissan in this way. When the EMEA marketing director wanted help to deliver a big speech at the Geneva Motor Show, we were brought in on the recommendation of his head of public relations. She had been in workshops with us and had seen us at work. She was also some-one in whom the EMEA marketing director had enormous confidence and she asked us to help him write and deliver the speech. It was a high-stakes, high-trust engagement – all his worldwide bosses would see his performance on stage as well as the world's media. When we met him for the first time, we hit it off. We both invested a lot of time to get it right and he delivered the speech from memory, word-perfect. We did the next five motor shows and are still friends.

Slow the hell down. Take it easy. The Japanese concept of speed is perfectly reflected in this proverb: 'Fast is slow, but continuously, without interruptions . . .'

If you are in a rush to close a deal, you will fail. You will look like you just don't get the prospective client's business cycle or understand their immediate concerns – what's on their mind right now – and as a consequence you will appear last-minute and incapable of planning well. Clients don't want to do busi-ness with or take advice from people like that.

Instead, build the relationship. One of the clients we spoke with tells of his experience in the USA. Having just moved from Britain to Atlanta to take on a big role at the Coca-Cola Corporation Global Headquarters, he arrived in the autumn. Having gone out ahead – his wife and family were yet to join him in the States – he was still living alone by Thanksgiving. Knowing that he was on his own in a new neighbourhood and new country at this very special time for family, the principal of an advisory firm who wanted to work with Coca-Cola very much, a man by the name of Pat, invited this client over to spend the holiday with his own family. Pat had intuited that the newcomer would be at a loss for what to do and alone on the biggest family holiday in the American calendar, and may not even know what the celebration was all about. He felt that this wasn't very neighbourly in the deeply hospitable southern state of Georgia. The invitation was accepted and the Brit never forgot the kindness that had been offered at a stressful time when he knew no one and was a stranger in a foreign land.

Pat, quite naturally, stayed in touch and tried to be useful as well as friendly until the time inevitably came when the now well-established Brit had a problem.

I must get Pat to look at this, the Brit thought. Of course he did. Pat had first sought to help and shown kindness. He would now profit.

Simon picks up on this theme: 'I was taken to the Monaco Grand Prix. And I took my son as well. These people had shown me kindness (they knew I wanted to go). Of course, it makes you predisposed. There is a sense of obligation. It didn't get them business but it did get them access and I always received them in the right mindset. It does work. It makes you predisposed to listen to what they have to say.'

They are wrong in Francis Ford Coppola's film *The Godfather*: it isn't ever 'strictly business, nothing personal'. Business is supremely personal and personal relationships take time to build. They start with the kindness of strangers. But that kindness shouldn't be random or thoughtless. It should be related to the person's interests. Be appropriate with your hospitality – if the person likes sport, then tickets to their team playing your team will be appreciated. If they hate sport but love grand settings and privileged access to places most people can't get into, or if they like to rub shoulders with the good and the great, get your local MP to host a dinner in the Palace of Westminster or run an event in an Oxford College or at Windsor Castle. (All of these things we have done, and you can do them too.)

Our clients are also unanimous in their observance of basic good manners. Unfortunately, too many people mistake talking for impressing. But conversation – especially social conversation – is a two-way interaction.

'People infrequently ask you questions,' complains a director at Barclays Bank. 'People have forgotten the art of being a good human being. By all means, tell me about you, but at least ask some questions about my world, show some interest – ask, "So what about you then?"'

We know a woman who was born totally deaf. She is an actress now. When she calls you on the phone – and she does – it is obviously going to be a one-way communication and when she calls it is usually because she needs to tell you something urgently. But even she understands the conventions of normal verbal discourse dictate that the other person must be given a chance to correspond. So she always asks how you are or what you're up to once she has told you what she needs to tell you. We asked her what she does on the other end of the phone when she has asked these questions.

'I ask the question and then I normally go quiet for about ten to fifteen seconds because that's normally enough for them to say how they are and so on. It makes it all more normal and then I can cut back in and say, "Nice to speak with you," and everyone goes away as if a normal chat has just happened.'

Our friend cannot hear a word that the other person is saying. But it is an important acknowledgement of the ritual that, in normal everyday life, we take for granted. In business, so often we are either oblivious to the fact that we are boring on and on, and failing to share the conversational to and fro. Or else – and just as catastrophically – we ask the question and, a bit like our friend, stand there for the period of time we think is appropriate, without really listening, and then we start up talking again. Guess how the person you are talking at feels about you now? Not great. In fact, she probably never wants to bump into you again.

'Have some manners!' is the cry from all clients. 'Ask some questions of me and about me. Don't just talk at me.'

3. Hunt in a pack and take your time

No big surprise, the bigger the prize, the longer it might take to land. It took Pat several years to get the nod on a project from Coca-Cola. It took the McLaren Formula 1 partnership team six years to get a deal with Vodafone. McLaren's long-serving CEO of marketing, Ekrem Sami, had been in contact with Vodafone's global marketing chief, David Haines, to try and do the multi-million-pound deal. Ekrem was unlucky and didn't get the business; the sponsorship deal was done with Ferrari instead. But Ekrem stayed in touch with David Haines and the Vodafone team and when the review came half a decade later, guess who was in pole position?

It wasn't just luck. Everything to do with the sponsorship had been very well thought through so that when the time came, it was, as some people like to say, 'oven-ready'. But there was more. In putting together a deal of this magnitude – or any magnitude – you need multiple advocates within the organisation. That is, you need to get buy-in from a variety of stakeholders.

In a typical firm with between one hundred and five hundred employees, an average of seven people are involved in most buying decisions.

A not insignificant voice in this deal was the Indian-American CEO of the entire global Vodafone Group, Arun Sarin. In the background to the main conversation between McLaren's team and the marketers at Vodafone, a relationship was being cultivated between Sarin and Ron Dennis, the mercurial CEO and prime driving force of McLaren. Arun let a thorough pitch process run and when the executive committee had voted positively in support of the sponsorship, he said his good friend Ron would be delighted. A good case of the sort of 'surround sound' – everybody at every level making the same noises – you need to land big deals. This is the kind of forethought and 'man-marking' that characterises great new business prospecting. It is the kind of world-class practice that circumnavigates the need to pitch formally for business. After all, who wants to be in a 'beauty parade'? It is also the correct way to use any influence you might have inside the client organisation. No instructions were issued from the top down that this meeting must happen or that person must be met.

Our friend Giorgio Belloli from the fashion company Farfetch echoes this sentiment: 'How long can it take to land a major fashion label to sign with us? For us, six to twelve months. It is a team effort on logistics to manage all the relationships that need to be managed. It is not a job for just one person.' Pack hunters tend to be more successful.

Another excellent example of pack hunting is KPMG. The big accounting firms and management consultancies like Bain and McKinsey sell incredibly large projects into their client firms with 'gob-smackingly' large fees attached. When David Wheldon was put on the executive committee at RBS, he was contacted by KPMG, who were consulting the bank at the time.

'Why would KPMG, want to meet with me, in marketing?' he pondered. 'I have nothing to do with the work they do for us as a company.' But David realised that KPMG – and many of the top consulting firms who operate at the highest level as professional advisors to the boards of major public limited companies – were 'man marking'. They knew that the work they conducted for RBS would be discussed at board level and that David, as a member of the board, would not only be involved in those discussions, but would also, crucially, have a say and a vote on work they were producing. It was therefore a strategic necessity for KPMG to get to know David, and for him to get to know them, and what they were seeking to accomplish for RBS. David was impressed with the thoroughness and forward-thinking determination to establish a working relationship across the board, not just within the narrow remit of their functional responsibility and day-to-day client. It demonstrated a deep, strategic understanding of how complex alliances lie at the heart of decision-making in big businesses.

But there was another reason why KPMG wanted to establish a relationship with David.

4. Seek to understand and then seek to help

KPMG start by getting to understand a business. Therefore, any perspective from within the business – from any discipline, however far removed from KPMG's own sphere of competence – adds to this overall understanding. The more they understand, the more they can help. The more they can help, the more value they provide to the client leadership team and the organisation and, therefore, the more revenue they will generate.

That's all very well for a player that is already ensconced in a relationship with a client – although it is remarkable how few advisory firms have such a well-structured network of touch points within their client organisations as KPMG does. But you haven't got into the company yet. You have no business with them yet.

Nor will you ever get through the door if your opening gambit is: 'Can you free up twenty minutes in your diary so we can tell you about this proprietary product we have?'

The person you are hoping to meet, to make a deal with, will be super busy. The area of business you specialise in will be a microscopically small part of their day job. So make your sales pitch interesting. Here, you have a number of options. If, like our friend Giorgio, you work in the space where fashion and technology meet, then you are on to a winner. When he was trying to fix meetings to meet the big fashion brands such as Gucci and Prada, they were all aware of and interested in the digital space and what it might mean for the future of their brands. But very few of these mega-brands had yet ventured into it or felt at home in this new world and marketplace. Giorgio was able to expose them to something they had heard about but didn't really understand at that time.

It always helps to strike up a dialogue when you have something genuinely new to say and to offer – especially if, like Giorgio, you have invested years getting to know the people who work inside your prospective client companies and they will always pick up the phone to you and give you time for a chat over a coffee.

But in many fields, you don't have that advantage. What do you do then?

Peter Mead, ex-vice chair of Omnicom and co-founder of Abbott Mead Vickers BBDO, one of the UK's largest advertising agencies, used to talk about 'the objectivity of ignorance'. By this, he meant the ability of a firm that is hunting for new business to use to its advantage its ignorance of the prospective client's company and the issues it faces. This sounds like a direct contradiction with what we have been saying about the need to use every information source at your disposal to find out everything you can in order to understand the client, their business and their industry to the best degree you can. But Mead meant that your ignorance is a protection. It is a protection because, unlike an incumbent advisor already working with this client organisation, you cannot be expected to know every detail about the company politics, the major internal issues at play, the track record of things they have tried or the current state of their thinking. Going in as an outsider – albeit a very well-read and well-prepared outsider – gives you licence to say things and ask questions, and to be forgiven for getting things wrong. This is a tremendously useful advantage you have over the incumbent. Where you will be forgiven, they will be expected to know, and thought badly of for not knowing.

Yet, how many times has the golden opportunity to impress been squandered? How many times has the chance to impress by exhibiting a grasp of the market and a viewpoint on the company's issues been thrown away with the lazy default to presenting your company's credentials? Company credentials should be banned. Banish the credentials deck (for it will be a PowerPoint presentation deck). Credentials presentations are the *bête noire* of the client community. Why? Because they are all about you and never about the client. In this age, we would have hoped that credentials decks would be a thing of the past. League tables showing where your organisation is relative to its peers, awards won, overblown case studies of the work done for clients, the ever-present map of the world showing where all your offices are. It is all, to clients, sickening.

Instead, come prepared to demonstrate your thinking and intelligence about the client and their business.

Sergio Zyman, the *enfant terrible* of the marketing world, used to ask companies wanting to do business with him to show him 'your worst case study and what you learned from it, your best case study and then give me a point of view on my brand', and he would then name a brand that might be having issues that needed a fresh perspective.

'But DON'T show me your credentials!' he finished.

David Wheldon recommends you 'start with questions, especially "How can we make the best use of your time?" And use the benefit of ignorance to make an educated guess and create a point of view.'

Time devoted to thinking about the client's business will normally yield at least a few original ideas, and if you are able to demonstrate that you have clearly invested effort into the meeting, you will leave a very favourable impression. We would also suggest that with a little perspicacious perspective, you will get to where they are currently in the process with the incumbent advisor. We have often heard prospective clients exclaim: 'It has taken our current advisor team over a year to get to this point of understanding about the core issue facing us. And you have only looked at it over the last few weeks. That's impressive.'

It seems impressive but it is often much easier than it appears. Many client organisations face many of the same problems you or your company will have experienced with other clients. Spotting patterns and making connections between unrelated sectors is the benefit of specialism. It is no coincidence that the big consulting firms do not recognise inherent conflict issues, and often service several or even a multitude of clients operating within the same industry. They see it as an advantage – it creates a body of expertise within their advisory capability.

If you make a mark on the first meeting discussing business, follow up. (Remember: keep showing up.) The client is bound to say things that provide a shopping list of needs or issues which you can go away and think through – and which, in the cause of being helpful, will provide you with an excuse for another meeting. Be like our colleague listening to the Unilever speech at the conference in Istanbul – try to catch the needs and cries for help as they spill out of the client's mouth. These are pearls for you to shine.

We should sound a note of caution here, however. The clients we spoke with are wise to people pretending that they can do everything.

'Can you help us with (problem goes here) will always be answered with "Yes!",' says one senior client. 'Regardless of whether they can or cannot. Don't be insincere or inauthentic. Know what you can do and have the grace to admit what you cannot do.'

By the same token, don't be supine or Uriah Heep-ish. Don't be craven or agree to do anything just to get a foothold (or, even worse, just to keep the client spending with you if you already work with them). How you start the relationship at the courting stage speaks volumes about you, and will set the tone. Don't make it a 'bended knee' relationship from the start. Being in the professional advisory business, you are in the client *service* business, not the *servile* business.

That said, know when to back off. Persistence pays, but play the long game. No one likes a pest. If you are getting knock back or definite 'back off' signals, then retreat gracefully and live to fight another day when, perhaps, the timing is more opportune. Just because you are in a hurry doesn't mean they have to be in a hurry too.

5. Don't make enemies: smile and keep going

New business is an emotional investment. If you chase someone and get the opportunity to pitch for their business but don't win it, it is tempting to get frustrated. A lot of midnight oil gets burnt chasing after elusive clients. But never show your frustration. It sounds platitudinous, but in the heat of the moment we are all capable of losing our cool and saying something to vent our feelings.

Don't.

You only need to keep going. To live and fight another day. Take bad news on the chin and refocus your efforts on bringing it in next time (remember McLaren and Vodafone). Continue to be helpful, continue to be enthusiastic, continue to court the attention of your intended.

Giorgio says:

> Always be kind and gentle. Treat everyone with respect. When we are approached by brands wanting to partner with us, we always treat everyone with respect, even if there is no immediate case for us to partner with them. We would always keep the door open – after all, brands change fortune every season and people move between brands and companies – so we will say things like, 'We are interested, but availability is an issue right now,' or, 'We are always open to opportunity, but this isn't a priority for us right now.'

This is a grand way of saying what the food stall owners in Marrakech's Jemaa el-Fnaa all say when you pass up on their invitation to eat at their food stall: 'Maybe later, yes?!' They make it easy for you when you reject their stall because they know you may be back later today or tomorrow, and tomorrow you may say 'yes'. We all need revenue tomorrow, not just today, so always keep the door ajar.

Keep the way open

In summary, doing all that these clients prescribe works. But it takes a particular mentality. In the world of sales and new business, the common parlance is to divide people into 'hunters' and 'farmers'. Hunters are, by tradition, red in tooth and claw salespeople who sniff out opportunity and go 'kill' the big beasts. They love the chase and treat it as a sort of glorified hunt for prey. Their terminology and demeanour are all about conquest and kills. By contrast, farmers are seen as people who nurture long-term relationships with clients, relationships which grow year on year. They are not hunter-killers; they are nurturers. People who push things forward every year, slowly, methodically and, maybe, a bit ploddingly.

Simon has a different way of looking at it. He doesn't think new business sales are served well by hunters. They wear their ambition and mission too nakedly. They want glory. They worship at the altar of closing rates – at the glory to be had by getting a sales scalp. When Simon used to work with the network of car dealerships in his company, he used to preach the gospel of what he calls 'diligent farmers'. It is his label that we adopted in our model and approach to describe our own philosophy of the ideal new business strategy. Simon understood new business as a pyramid. For him, the focus of effort must be on building the base of the pyramid. The base of the pyramid is where all the embryonic, potential customers are brought into the process.

'Talk to me about the base of your sales pyramid, not your sales peak at the top of the pyramid,' he would command his dealer network. He wanted them to build robust relationships at the base, a regular cycle of potential customer visits – and this takes time and effort and patience. It is not work that appeals to hunters, who want their fix – and their fix is for closed sales. Build the base and you will create a constant and rich stream of prospect customers moving up the pyramid towards purchase. The more prospects you create at the base and the more you nurture and herd them up the pyramid, the more sales will result at the top. By the time these prospects get to the top of the purchase pyramid, their custom should be a certainty. If you have done your job thoroughly and well, and looked after them through the preceding few years, you will be rewarded with a sale. Lots of sales. Lots more than if you just focus on the people at the top of the pyramid (the people wanting to buy now) where you have built no loyalty or affinity with the prospective customer and where it is a bit of a lottery as to which brand they will buy.

Be a diligent farmer. It works. Don't be a hunter – they will see you coming and then they will run a mile.

CHAPTER 7

BUILDING RAPID RAPPORT

'I am an unpopular electric eel set in a pond of catfish'
Edith Sitwell

Edith Sitwell, the British poet, critic and eccentric who died in the mid-1960s, once described herself thus. Anyone who's worked with people knows that sometimes, despite your best efforts, the chemistry doesn't work – you're the electric eel and the catfish ain't buying.

Destructive personality clashes get in the way of catalysing growth – people tend to buy from people they like, and they tend to like people who are *like* them. It's a basic rule of selling. But personality clashes are easy to avoid. Being aware of other people's behavioural styles gives you the information you need to adapt your behaviour with people who are different from you, so you get on with them better. And if you get on with them better, they will remember you, think of you positively, be predisposed to listen to you, meet with you again and, ultimately, to receive your recommendations more receptively. You will be able to communicate with them in the language they speak and style they use. Lo and behold, you have personal chemistry.

In any first meeting, you want to be able to build rapport rapidly between you and the other person. Having the ability to identify quickly what type of person you might be dealing with helps accelerate that rapport. How do you do it?

There are many well-documented psychological tests to identify the different behavioural styles that people have. The system we prefer divides people into four major archetypes. We like this number. It keeps things simple and easy to remember, and none of the other, more complicated models have ever helped us more than this one. It is a very practical tool. It is also beneficial to remember that most of us have one dominant behavioural style and one subsidiary. So we tend to operate most of the time according to the characteristics of our dominant style. This means that people who have dominant behavioural styles that aren't the same as our own will find us challenging to deal with – without meaning to or without us meaning to either. It's just that the four styles are different, and people in one style group want and need different things and ways of being treated than people in another. It explains why birds of a feather tend to flock together, and why sometimes, when you meet someone who isn't your style, well, you might feel they're not exactly your 'type'.

The test is based on a self-completed questionnaire which gets each person to choose one out of four possible alternative answers in describing their own strengths and weaknesses. However, once you become adept at spotting the telltale signs that people exhibit, you won't need them to fill out a questionnaire; you will be able to decipher which style is their dominant one through simple observation and acute listening.

Back to the questionnaire: there are twenty sets of four adjectives in strengths and another twenty sets of four adjectives in weaknesses. You pick one adjective in each set of four choices. Once the person has completed these, the answers are compiled into four columns, each column representing one of the four different behavioural styles. The higher the number of answers in a given column, the more prone you are to behave, communicate and see the world as others with that dominant behavioural style would. Most people have two high-numbered columns and two lower-numbered columns; usually one of the two is slightly higher in number than the other. The highest-numbered column is your dominant style. The second highest-numbered column is your secondary style. So most people find at least two styles pretty comfortable. A few people have a close to even spread across all four columns. All this means is that they find it relatively easy to get on with anyone in any of the four styles.

In essence, this methodology divides the world into quarters:

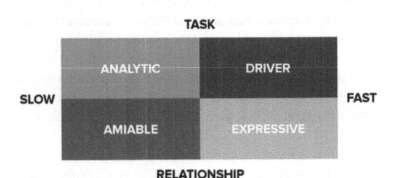

At the top, there are people for whom the task is the most important priority. At the bottom are the people for whom the relationship is the priority. They are not mutually exclusive, just differentiated by degree of importance. On the right of the grid are people who prefer to 'tell' or to move at speed. On the left of the grid are people who prefer to 'ask' and who work more deliberately and slowly. Going clockwise, you have:

Fast, task-oriented people – they are called Drivers.
Fast, relationship-oriented people – they are called Expressives.

Slow, relationship-oriented people – they are called Amiables.

Slow, task-oriented people – they are called Analyticals.

Here's how the four different types tend to see themselves:

Drivers: Exacting, efficient, determined, direct and decisive. Have little time for social niceties. Want to get on with it, to get the job done, the task completed. Hate debates that go round in circles. Want to get things sorted. They hate not being in control more than anything else in the world.

Expressives: Energetic, creative, open, optimistic and quick on their feet. Easily bored and don't like detail. Impulsive. Need to be stimulated. Enjoy the limelight. Work fast, like to tell people their views and need to be the centre of attention.

Amiables: Warm, accepting, patient, cooperative, friendly and non-confrontational. Like to build consensus (slowly). Good at building long-term relationships. Like to ensure people are comfortable and feel heard. They are life's natural diplomats. They loathe and seek to avoid confrontation at all costs.

Analyticals: Precise, careful, reserved, logical. Will not be hurried. Make decisions based on fact and evidence, not supposition and hunch. Don't like showiness. Methodical and slower in their processes as they have a horror of getting something (anything) wrong. For them, it is all about avoiding mistakes.

Health warning

However, there is often a marked disparity between the way we see ourselves and the way that others perceive us. The effect these four groups have on each other and on people who are not like them can be alarming. So it pays to understand how each group appears from the outside of that group. This is how they look from the outside:

Drivers: Usually seen by other groups as autocratic, critical, demanding, insensitive and domineering (Drivers don't necessarily see this as negative, nor do they really care that much what others feel about them – at least, not on the surface). If you get two Drivers trying to run a meeting, you're in trouble. They'll both be competing with each other for control of the room. Drivers believe if it wasn't for them, nothing would get done. Everyone else wishes they'd stop trying to boss everyone around and listen.

Expressives: Can be seen as pushy, superficial, prone to exaggerate with no follow through and overconfident. They are especially irritating to Analyticals because they are so emotional. Expressives fizz about and fall in love with the last great idea they heard about. Naturally enthusiastic, they believe they are the ideas brigade. They believe there'd be no new ideas if it wasn't for them. Everyone else wishes they'd calm down.

Amiables: Can often be viewed as weak, time-wasting (all that touchy-feely small talk before getting down to business), lacking goals and slow to make decisions. Amiables irritate the hell out of Drivers. But Amiables can knit relationships together and tend to look at the long-term. Everyone wishes they'd stop asking how everyone's feeling and get to the job in hand. Oh, and be on time.

Analyticals: Tend to be seen (especially by Expressives) as stubborn, nit-picking, perfectionist, pedantic and unemotional. Again, this type of person wears such labels with pride. After all, if they didn't dot the i's and cross the t's, who would? Other groups can find their pace glacial and their aversion to taking risks frustrating. Everyone else wishes they would see the wood, not just the trees.

Is it manipulative to flex your style in order to build better rapport? Are we asking you to abandon your own personality and become chameleon-like, inhabit a netherworld or identity which morphs from one type wholly into another? No. We are only interested in helping you get your message across effectively. You can use these insights to get a sense of who's across the table from you and how to best communicate with them – couching your idea, your solution, in a way that has the greatest chance of being understood by the prospect. It puts your thinking into their language and removes any distractions that could get in the way. Additionally, most of us have at least two of the four behavioural styles and at least a smattering of the remaining two. Think of it like a graphic equaliser: you dial up some attributes and dial down the others. Being aware of how each of the behavioural styles behave just gives you more options for how to communicate with them.

In the end, it turns out that the electric eel is not related to true eels but is a member of the neotropical knifefish order, which is actually more closely related to the catfish. With a bit of effort, we bet they'd find they had lots in common after all.

HOW TO BUILD RAPID RAPPORT THROUGH UNDERSTANDING BEHAVIOURAL STYLES

Any Drivers reading this will probably skip this bit. 'Yeah, yeah,' they'll say to themselves, 'I get it.' On to the next chapter. Consequently, they will miss out on a lot of very useful information about how to get more of what they want in life out of their relationships, but, hey-ho, it's their choice.

For those of you who want a bit more detail on the secret of building rapid rapport, on increasing the chemistry between you and others leading on to catalysing more new business, read on. Which is, after all, the whole point of this book. But that's the problem with Drivers: sometimes they are so busy being efficient, they forget to be effective.

Having got this far, you'll know we are evangelists for being 'interested and interesting' – code for the core skill of all great communicators. Which is to 'know thyself', and to use the senses to pick up signals from others in order to adapt behaviour to build better rapport. Knowing yourself allows you to adapt to the world of others – it gives you the option not to be the raw, undiluted you, but to be cleverer, more sensitive to the needs of others. And you need to be. If three-quarters of the planet's population aren't like you (the four behavioural styles are more or less equally spread in the population), then you need to meet people in a way that mitigates against conflict arising between the different types. There is inherent conflict built into these different types when they meet.

We're not saying that if you are a Driver and you meet an Amiable, there is no chance of any chemistry between you and you might as well get your coat straight away. What we are saying is that you may find it harder – especially in a business context – to find common ground quickly. When it comes to new business and first meetings, often you don't have the luxury of time. Which is where understanding behavioural styles can be useful. It allows you to spot what 'type' of person you may be dealing with and adjust your behaviour as a result to avoid losing potential business just by being yourself.

It's important to note here that everyone, of course, is a unique individual. No one can easily be put into a box and their personality captured. But we do know there are some traits that can help diagnose how we *typically* behave, and that we can identify those broad traits in others. Which is a useful tool if you are seeking to create chemistry between you and another person who perhaps doesn't see the world the way you see it.

As we have said, of the four archetypes, Expressives and Amiables are more people-orientated, while Drivers and Analyticals are more task-orientated. Between the Expressives and the Amiables, the Expressives operate fast and the Amiables like to take their time. The Expressives prefer to tell you, the Amiables prefer to ask you. On the other side, the Drivers work more quickly and the Analyticals are slower and more deliberate. The Drivers definitely prefer to tell you, and the Analyticals are more prone to asking questions or for permission.

Buying style characteristics

DRIVER
Typical characteristics:
- Highly interested in new products and innovations
- Usually possess a fairly high ego factor
- Does not like to waste time

Type of sales presentation required:
- Don't waste their time
- They don't want lots of facts and figures. Hit the high points. Get to the 'bottom line'
- Can be difficult to move from present, trusted suppliers, but, once switched, they will remain highly loyal as long as you provide the service
- Will not want to see many testimonials, research data, etc., but may delegate this to a subordinate
- Be concise and businesslike. Don't waste time with idle talk. Get to the point quickly, solve problems fast and make the sale

EXPRESSIVE
Typical characteristics:

- Friendly, people-orientated person who would usually rather talk and socialise than do detailed work
- Will be glad to see you arrive; will trade jokes and stories readily. Won't want to discuss business too much; will prefer telling stories and talking about other things
- Likes to try out new and innovative products

Type of sales presentation required:

- Spare the details; the Expressive will not want to hear them – hit the high notes
- Often, will buy easily from you with only a minimum presentation but beware: the competition can steal them away from you just as easily. They fall in love with the last idea they hear
- So give plenty of follow-up on service
- Talk new products. Socialise

AMIABLE
Typical characteristics:

- May be a little shy but wants to be your friend
- Not as suspicious as the Analytical but still very slow to make changes
- Usually a hard worker who puts priorities on things other than appearances

Type of sales presentation required:

- Take it slow and easy; if you try to rush them, you will lose the sale
- Provide plenty of proof and statistics
- Earn their trust and friendship, learn about family and hobbies

- May require additional visits for reassurances before the sale is made
- Emphasise your proven products
- Make repeat calls. Be sure all questions are answered

Typical characteristics:

- May be suspicious of you and your products
- Does not make changes to new suppliers easily
- Usually not too talkative
- Is not an 'innovator', will not readily try out new and innovative technology

Type of sales presentation required:

- Don't rush. Don't waste time with small talk. Present sitting down across a table using a fact-checked document; give them physical space to be objective
- Get right to the point with plenty of facts
- Needs lots of 'proof' background information and proven results before buying
- Needs to take time, absorb details and digest facts before going on to next step
- Highly suspicious of new and unproven products; use testimonials or plenty of research information to back up your presentation
- Testimonials work ... from other Analytical types
- Be sure all questions are answered comprehensively

Checklists for role shifting

DRIVERS
Do:

- Be clear, specific, brief and to the point

- Stick to business
- Come prepared with all requirements, objectives and support material in a well-organised 'package'
- Present your facts logically; plan your presentation efficiently
- Ask specific questions
- Provide alternatives and choices for them to make their own decisions
- Provide facts and figures about the probability of success or effectiveness of options
- If you disagree, take issues with the facts not the person
- Motivate and persuade by referring to objectives and results
- Support their conclusions
- After talking business, make a quick leave-taking

Don't:
- Ramble on, waste time or hang on for a personal chat after finishing business
- Try to build a personal relationship
- Be disorganised, messy or forget things
- Confuse or distract their mind from business
- Leave loopholes or vague issues if you do not want to be put down
- Ask rhetorical or irrelevant questions
- Direct, order or tell them what to do
- Come with a ready-made decision and do not make it for them
- Speculate wildly or offer guarantees and assurances where there is uncertainty about meeting them
- Let disagreements reflect upon them personally
- Reinforce points you agree on with, 'I will support you'
- Try to convince by 'personal' means

EXPRESSIVES

Do:

- Support their dreams and intuitions
- Leave time for socialising
- Talk about people and their objectives; offer opinions they find stimulating
- Commit them to courses of actions
- Ask for their opinions and ideas about people
- Provide ideas for carrying out decisions
- Use enough time to be stimulating, fun-loving, fast-moving
- Offer incentives for quick action and risk-taking

Don't:

- Lay down the law or suppress their opinions
- Be curt, cold or tight-lipped
- Concentrate on facts and figures, alternatives, abstractions or go into detail
- Leave decisions up in the air
- 'Dream' with them or you will lose time
- Mess around too much or stick rigidly to the agenda
- Talk down to them, do not patronise
- Be dogmatic

AMIABLES

Do:

- Start, however briefly, with a personal comment – break the ice
- Show sincere interest in them as people; find areas of common involvement; be candid and open
- Patiently draw out personal objectives and work with them to help achieve these; listen, be responsive
- Present your case softly, without threat
- Ask 'how' questions to draw out their opinions

- Watch carefully for possible areas of early disagreement or dissatisfaction
- If you disagree, look for personal reasons such as hurt feelings
- Behave casually, informally
- Define clearly (preferably in writing) individual contributions
- Provide guarantees that their decision will minimise risks; give assurances and emphasise the benefits
- Provide personal assurances with clear, specific solutions with maximum guarantees

Don't:
- Rush headlong into business or agenda
- Stick solely to business, but don't lose sight of goals by being too personal
- Force them to respond quickly to your objectives; do not say, 'This is how I see the situation'
- Be domineering or demanding; do not threaten them with position power
- Debate about facts and figures
- Manipulate or bully them into agreeing because they probably will not fight back
- Patronise or demean them by using subtlety or invective
- Be abrupt and rapid
- Be vague; do not offer options and responsibilities
- Offer assurances and guarantees you cannot fill
- Keep deciding for them or then leave them without support

ANALYTICALS
Do:
- Prepare your 'case' in advance
- Approach them in a straightforward, direct way; stick to business

- Support their principles; use a thoughtful approach; build your credibility by listing pros and cons to any suggestions you make
- Present specific recommendations and deliver what you say you can do
- Take time but be persistent
- Draw up a scheduled approach to implementing action with a step-by-step timetable; assure them there will be no surprises
- If you agree, follow through
- If you disagree, make an organised presentation of your position
- Give them time to verify reliability of your actions, be accurate, realistic
- Provide solid, tangible, practical evidence
- Minimise risk by providing guarantees over a period of time
- When appropriate, give them time to be thorough

Don't:
- Be disorganised or messy
- Be giddy, casual, informal, loud
- Rush the decision-making process
- Be vague about what is expected of either of you; do not fail to follow through
- Leave things to chance or luck
- Threaten, cajole, wheedle, coax
- Use testimonials of others or unreliable sources
- Use someone's opinion as evidence
- Use gimmicks or clever quick manipulations
- Push too hard or be unrealistic with deadlines

CLOSING TECHNIQUES

After all that talking, you now need to bring things to a conclusion. Getting clients to take action is the most sensitive part of the whole process because this is when they actually have to commit, to *do* something. The way you do that is to 'close' the conversation or meeting by using closing techniques. Closing techniques are specific ways in which you ask the client to take action.

Some closing techniques work more effectively than others on certain behavioural types. If you get the right one, it will tip the playing field your way. If you get the wrong one, you could end up back at square one. Although there are many ways to 'close' a conversation, there are five common closing techniques. Here they are:

Confident/direct close: This is the most direct way to ask for concrete action to be taken.

'Shall we start next week?'

Summary close: This close ends the conversation with a recap of the two or three big reasons why action should be taken.

'Let me restate the three major reasons to do this project: 1, 2, 3.'

Alternative close: Beloved of car salespeople the world over, this close posits two alternative courses of action – but precludes the possibility of taking no action.

'Would you like this model in blue or red?'

Fear close: A close which points out the consequences of taking no action. Much beloved of every trade practitioner in the world: plumbers, builders, electricians – anyone involved in putting things right that have gone wrong.

'My concern is that if we don't act now, this situation will change for the worse and that means you will potentially lose your heating/hot water/boiler/electricity/house. Acting now will prevent that happening. But it's up to you.'

Concession close: Makes everything bite-sized – breaks down the commitment being asked for into smaller, mini-commitments.

'Instead of doing the whole project immediately, why don't we break it down into phases, starting with a test market phase in one region only, which we can begin immediately?'

To put it in layman's terms, children use these five closing techniques all the time. They will escalate to the next one if they are not achieving what they want. For example, if they want to go to the playground, they start with the confident close: 'Dad, get your coat, we're going to the playground.'

If that doesn't get the desired response, they move to option two, the summary close: 'Here are three good reasons why we should go to the playground right now: 1. It's sunny; 2. We'll get some exercise; and 3. It'll be fun!'

Still no dice? Move to DEFCON 3: the alternative close: 'OK. Either we go to the playground, or we go to the toy shop – the choice is yours.'

Still you resist. Undeterred, they wheel out the fear close: 'If you don't take me to the playground, I will run around the house shouting and never leave you alone.'

Now you're teetering on the brink. Will this child never give up? (In case you're wondering: the answer is no.) Here comes the concession close: 'Tell you what, Dad. Let's go to the playground for fifteen minutes. If we like it and we're having fun, we'll stay. If not, we'll come straight home *and get an ice cream on the way.*' (Note the addition of the additional need creation and implied threat.)

And if all else fails, they will resort, just like you and me, to the 'puppy dog' close: 'Pleeeease, Dad!'

Irresistible.

Each of these closing techniques work well, but some work better with Expressives than they do with Analyticals, and some work better with Amiables than Drivers. Can you work out which is best to use with each behavioural style? And which closing technique would definitely *not* work with each style? Remember what each style values the most:

- Expressives want to act, and they hate the idea of missing out on anything; they would rather do something than nothing.
- Drivers want control over the decision.
- Analyticals want to get it right – their worst nightmare is to make a mistake.
- Amiables have a hard time taking action because they want consensus, and they want to avoid conflict.

	USE	DON'T USE
AMIABLE	CONFIDENT	ALTERNATIVE

Amiables have a hard time committing to action. At least try and get them to do so by demonstrating certainty and attempting to push them into action. If you give them options, you will put them in a spin and they won't be able to decide between the options without canvassing opinion. They will be stuck in a miasma of indecision.

	USE	DON'T USE
DRIVER	ALTERNATIVE	FEAR

Drivers like choice, or at least they need to have the illusion of choice. Posing two or more potential routes and asking them to choose which one they prefer gives them the power they so earnestly seek. You would be ill-advised to use a fear close with them because they will feel they are being effectively blackmailed, or forced into a corner. If you force a Driver into a corner, she will come out fighting.

	USE	DON'T USE
ANALYTICAL	SUMMARY	CONCESSION

Analyticals want to get it right and they value having the options laid out before them for objective inspection. A summary close reprises the logical arguments for taking action – it lists the reasons this is the right thing to do. One caveat: once you have summarised, shut up. Don't put these people under pressure; they need space and time to evaluate and hate high-pressure 'sales-y-ness'. With Analyticals, as we mentioned, it is often best to sit down with a table between you because they value having physical distance between themselves and the 'other party' (yep, they really do refer to other people as 'other parties' – everything is impersonal). That way, they can evaluate facts without the proximity of personality. Conversely, don't try to con them by offering a concession close; they will see it as a con. If they are not yet convinced of the merits of what you are proposing, why would they commit to starting work on a part of it? For them, that just doesn't make logical sense.

	USE	DON'T USE
EXPRESSIVE	ALL OF THEM EXCEPT...	... SUMMARY

Expressives live for excitement. They want to get on with doing stuff, they want to take action. They loathe the idea that they might miss out on something. So, of all the four different types, they are the ones most likely to go with your proposal. The only closing technique they won't respond positively to is the summary close. Why are you repeating the arguments for doing this again? they will be thinking. You had me at 'Hello' – now you're boring me.

HOW DO YOU SPOT WHICH BEHAVIOURAL STYLE SOMEONE IS WITHOUT THEM FILLING IN THE QUESTIONNAIRE?

If you look at someone's LinkedIn profile, the issues and interests they follow and contribute to, the words they use to describe themselves, whether or not they have changed the background picture from the standard template of the profile page etc., you will rapidly form a picture of who you are dealing with.

You are looking and listening for clues as to which of the four styles this person might adopt. It's not an exact science but you can generally work out the person's style preference from their LinkedIn profile or several sentences into a phone call or meeting. Most people are a combination of two dominant styles and weak on the other two. You should be able to work out what they are most likely to be – or at least which half of the matrix they are in – relatively fast. The big thing to try to spot is if they are top or bottom – top is the task-oriented people: Drivers and Anlyticals; bottom is the relationship-oriented people: Expressives and Amiables.

For example, if you are looking for clues in their LinkedIn profile, look how they comment on posts: do they leave short comments or long? What does that reveal about what they are interested in? For example, a post we made got two comments, one from a Driver and the other from an Amiable:

Driver:

Business life skills are so valuable and this is a cracking list of advantages to share.

Note the emphasis on value, list (Drivers like lists) and 'advantages' – all classic driver obsessions: achievement, practicality and competitive. It is also short and to the point, with no unnecessary words at all. The focus is all *task*; no mention of people or relationships. This is an old colleague of ours – his page on LinkedIn is all pure Driver.

Compare this to the Amiable-Analytic:

> Sadly, my own daughter's a little past the age when she'll be able to benefit from this advice. But I'm sure, coming from someone with your pedigree, that it will be a belting course and entirely devoid of piffle.

Note the longer sentences, more familial language, more personal tone. But this person has a high Analytical bent as well. You know this because of the underlying point: benefit (not an amiable word because it is about gain) and pedigree – track record/credibility.

This person's profile also has a nice photo backdrop of greenery and leaves. Very Amiable. But it's not just to look nice and friendly; it serves a purpose (Analytical secondary personality style): his company is called SpringThinking. The image has a specific, logical role.

Here's another Driver profile on LinkedIn:

> A Portfolio NED with blue chip executive experience, bringing devotion to the customer, brands, data and digital to the top table. Inspiring, incisive and refreshing.

All short and to the point: performance, contribution, achievement.

An example of an Analytical client whose profile on LinkedIn contains the bare minimum. He has a formal photo. His biography – the 'About' section – is a personality-free list of accomplishments, qualifications and speciality skills. It is all about proving his credentials. The background behind his picture is the standard one LinkedIn provides – as it is for the Drivers. They don't care for the personalisation of their page because, for them, that is vacuous imagery and therefore unimportant. If you look at the profile on LinkedIn for an Expressive, you will see that she has tailored photos which show her talking at events with lots of famous media brand names behind her. The Expressive is all about projecting an image – famous, important. The profile photo will be posed, stylish, often black and white to project style and professionalism. For Expressives, the company they keep says everything you need to know – so on the profile there will be a good selection of photos of them on stage or speaking on a panel of well-known luminaries. They are also easy to identify when you tell them about the personality styles as they will ask, 'What am I, then?' Dead giveaway!

If you have your radar on, it's a cinch to work out what sort of person you are dealing with, and once you know that, the chemistry between you should catalyse nicely and rapidly.

In terms of how that plays out in the virtual world, it is just the same. Living our lives 'on screen' suits all four types.

For the Drivers, it gives the illusion of being in control. Drivers, as we know, love to be in control. They can turn the camera on or off, mute people mid-sentence, retain exclusive control of the hosting and so deny everyone else freedom to play with the controls, change their background image or have any spontaneous fun. And operating virtually is efficient with time (no wasted time travelling or with small talk). Driver heaven.

Analyticals like it because it gives them the one thing they cherish more than anything else: physical distance from other units of humanity so they can listen attentively and think without others crowding their personal space or having to pretend to enjoy being in a room with real people.

Amiables like it because, well, it's just lovely to see everyone and meet up, isn't it?

Expressives love it because *they're on telly*! And every Expressive loves a stage. Lights, camera, action: it's showtime. And showtime is an Expressive's favourite time. They love an audience.

The screen makes everyone happy because it lets us be who we are and edit our world to suit ourselves. In the real world, we have to try to meet people halfway, play by their rules, listen to them drone on and on, dress up smart, be on our best behaviour.

On screen, things are perfect. In the real world, they're messy and unpredictable. Safe in our home TV studios, we can all be the amazing people we wish we were and wish other people to see. The one drawback is that videoconferencing is exhausting. Especially if you are in charge of the meeting. The need to stay focused, to watch and listen intently, with only limited access to real physical feedback (verbal and non-verbal), if any at all (many people mute or shut down their camera) can be very draining. Zooming has many advantages. And people get used to the protocols quickly. However, it might be best to limit the amount of time you do it per day as it is quite enervating for certain personality types.

CHAPTER 8

SUMMARY AND WHAT TO EXPECT FROM PART III

Focus on how you make them feel

TV and cinema are full of examples of great (new) business practices. One of the best is *The Simpsons*. Every episode is chock-full of brilliant human insight dressed up as comedy. In one episode, where Bart is doing jail time, he pals up with a delinquent girl who teaches him how to talk to people. She gives him only two things to say which will create instant rapport and help other people relate to you. The first piece of advice is to express empathy when someone is telling you something: 'If the person is telling you something intimate or important for them or about them, just say: "That must have been hard for you?"'

The second piece of advice is to follow up with, 'Tell me more.' Genius.

This is the secret of all empathisers – it puts you on their side and it gets the other person talking. How hard is that? But don't be a cynic – if you're genuinely not interested and you're just chasing the money, the insincerity will show. Also, a note of caution: certain of the four personality types we covered earlier will struggle to create empathy in this way. It just isn't in the nature of Drivers to be empathetic or even interested in how other people are feeling. But being good at new business requires you to learn new skills, right? So get some empathy and get empathising! If you do empathise and show you are interested, you are beginning a relationship that might last a lifetime. The clients we started out helping, the ones we really liked and who we got on with, turned into lifelong friends.

Listen, really listen to them. Turn on your 'radar'

David Meister was an Englishman who had a job at Harvard Business School in the town of Cambridge in the Commonwealth of Massachusetts. He was an esteemed academic and author of several highly acclaimed books. In order to work in the USA, as an alien, he needed a green card. His aunt – also English – also lived in the Commonwealth of Massachusetts on a green card. Very sadly, whilst David Meister was working in Harvard, his aunt died. As her only living relative in the USA, it fell to David to sort out the arrangements. David did what most people would do: he went to Google and searched for funeral directors. He started calling them. The first few all took the same approach and, after expressing their condolences for his loss, got straight down to business: what kind of casket (coffin) did he want? What sort of handles – brass or another metal? What was his budget? They were not trying very hard, were looking at this issue as a simple transaction and rushing to solve his problem with the certain expectation of a sale at the end of it – after all, he had to bury her, right? The next number he tried took a different approach. This time, the voice on the other end was attached to someone with a brain who had their radar turned on: 'Forgive me, sir,' said the funeral director on the other end of the phone, 'but do I detect a foreign accent? Are you, by any chance, not a US citizen but a resident alien in the United States?'

'You are correct,' replied David.

'And your aunt, the deceased, was she a resident alien as well – was she also from overseas?'

'Also correct,' replied David.

'Then, sir, you need to be aware that there are certain formalities and protocols pertaining to the death of a person of alien origin here in the Commonwealth of Massachusetts. Would it be helpful if I sent those over to you?'

This person helped David Meister. He went further. Made the effort to help him understand what was required to do this thing properly. The others – the competition – just had $ signs in their eyes and were eager for the sale rather than the trust of this potential client. Guess who got the business?

David Meister concludes from this episode a golden rule of new business:

Stop selling. Start helping.

Be of use. Be of service. Once again, a reminder: your self-interest is best served by serving others' best interests.

Do as you would be done by

It never ceases to amaze us how some people speak to receptionists (or anyone in a service role) with hostility and expect great things in return. If someone was rude or obnoxious to you, wouldn't it make you feel like doing the bare minimum rather than 'going the extra mile'? And yet, it happens all the time. Treat the receptionist with the same respect you treat the CEO – it really shouldn't need to be something you have to think about. When Louisa got her first job out of college, someone gave her some great advice: 'The two most important people in the company are the receptionist and the finance assistant. One will make sure you get your calls and the other will make sure you get paid.' Wise words.

Ask more questions

One of the reasons we encourage people to 'hunt in packs' – i.e., not go to meetings on your own – is that listening is hard work. Listening acutely to what's being said, writing it down, reading between the lines of what is being said as well as the literal meaning – it's a lot. You want to be asking lots of questions and really listening to the answers. If you have a colleague with you who will do the writing down bit, that's something off your mental load. And that colleague is likely to catch something that you don't – another advantage of not being alone.

Prospects are people too

The game of new business generation is a game of giving in order to receive – or at least in hope that you will receive. There is no guarantee. Certainly, you should not have an expectation that you will receive if you give – that way lies disappointment and also a counterproductive attitude. New business is not a simple transaction – if I do this then you must do that. Thinking that life is just a transaction is anathema to the spirit of how new business actually works. Yes, there is a reciprocity in the process – a feeling in the prospect that they might feel obliged to do something for you if you have done something for them (it is only human to do so), but you must not rely on it. Once you let them know they are obliged, you break the trust you are seeking to establish. Establishing trust is essential to building a long-term relationship with someone.

Too many people, who either don't 'get' how new business works, or who are in too great a hurry to close a deal, screw it up by rushing their fences. They rush straight from identifying a problem or a need the prospective client might have to proffering a solution (that will cost money and deliver revenue). Result: rejection.

Do your research with prospects – be really well prepared. But, as well as understanding the business in which they operate, make the effort to understand what's really going on in the world of the person you are courting. If you do this, and you do this consistently, you are already halfway there and you will be way, way ahead of your competition. Put yourself in their shoes. Stop regarding everything from your own narrow interests.

Use behavioural profiling to help you build better rapport more quickly

Again, all part of having your radar switched on. The more you look for clues, the more practised you will get at establishing what type of person you might be dealing with. If you're not confident that you're picking up the signals correctly with prospects, start with your family and friends. Observe your nearest and dearest. Start with their body language – how do they sit or stand? Are they expressive with their hands? Do they make eye contact? What about the way they talk? Do they speak quickly and cover a lot of ground or give short, sharp answers? Are they impatient or do they go into long, drawn-out descriptions? Make your own assumption and then ask the person to read the archetype descriptions and choose the one they think best describes how they behave. If you had made the same assumption, you're on the way to mastering this skill. And if you got it wrong, what was it that put you on the wrong track? Remember, most of us have at least two of the four behavioural styles and at least a smattering of the other two, so it's not always easy to get it right, particularly if a person is well-balanced across all of the styles. Keep practising, keep your radar on and soon your ability to 'spot the style' will become instinctive.

WHAT TO EXPECT FROM PART III

We hope, by now, that we have persuaded you of the benefits to being a catalyst and the importance of personal chemistry in business development. Parts III and IV focus on the practical – how can you set your company up to have a new business culture that is active rather than passive? How can you turn your contacts into contracts?

In Part III we'll focus on overcoming the barriers that often get in the way of new business success and outline how important it is to be clear on what you are selling so that you make it easy to buy. We make a case for the importance of the written word in communications and provide some tools and tips to turbocharge your pipeline and get more leads. Our emphasis is on the practical – providing you with practical approaches to going out and getting more work.

CULTURE: SETTING UP FOR NEW BUSINESS SUCCESS

CHAPTER 9

OVERCOMING THE BARRIERS

'Several excuses are always less convincing than one'
Aldous Huxley

In any organisation, the new business effort must be directed from the top and wholeheartedly embraced by the CEO. If it isn't, you are wasting your time. We know from experience that organisations will do anything and everything to sabotage themselves with turf wars and office politics. Egos are everywhere and unless they are forcibly kept in check by the CEO, no new business effort will ever succeed. We have seen shockingly bad behaviour by supposedly grown-up people from companies all over the world which just gets in the way of new business success. It can take many forms:

- Trying to subdue everyone to the will of an overmighty subject (turf wars);
- Passive resistance (saying you will comply and then simply not doing what you said you would);
- Behind-the-scenes briefing to your most senior line manager to escalate your view over other views or just downright rejection of authority (politicking and jostling for supremacy).

The only way to combat all of this playpen politicking is for the CEO to take a visible lead in exhibiting the desired behaviour around new business and to stamp on any misbehaviour. Indulgence of bad behaviour will undo all efforts and make the whole new business enterprise unsuccessful. Believe us. We have seen it happen. We are not saying that the CEO must do the day-to-day leadership of the new business effort. That job goes to another. But the CEO must be actively involved and provide intellectual focus so that everyone within the organisation knows they must comply.

Who does lead the effort day to day? A properly organised new business effort must be originated, administered and policed by an intelligent board-level director who has the respect of the whole team and the very visible backing of the CEO. It cannot be delegated to a middle manager. This person must be someone who can talk peer to peer with both senior colleagues and senior clients. Someone who is not fazed by internal resistance to new ways of doing things; who is more tenacious than the most belligerent senior colleague; who does not seek, but will not shirk, a fight when politicking rears its head; who is creative and disciplined; who commands the respect of the organisation; who has a track record in business development; and who is also charming, beguiling and fun, and who knows, without fail, that she always has the CEO's backing if she asks for it.

Frankly, these people are as rare as hen's teeth but keep looking. You need one of them. You could even be one of them. They, or you, will transform your organisation's business development and make your life busier but more profitable in the long run.

As for the CEO, she needs to inculcate an atmosphere of the highest intellectual expectations. It needs to be understood that when people present their proposals to her, they had better be (a) prepared for the encounter; and (b) have really interrogated their own presentation. It is the role of the CEO in new business to be the backbone of the enterprise – to insist on the highest performance. It needs to be understood that anything that falls short will incur the wrath and displeasure of the leadership. New business is unstinting and unforgiving. You may not like it, but it is so, nevertheless. Dissent and politicking cannot be tolerated. The stakes are too high.

WHAT GETS IN THE WAY?

How does it feel when you are given a hard financial target for your new business growth? Scary, huh? Let's say your shareholder – that private equity company who cosied up to you a year ago and is now looking for an exit in two more years – tells you that you have to double in size by the end of the year after next. Your current revenue is $40m. That means you need to be generating $80m. That's a lot of money. Especially as it took you seven years to get to your current revenue level.

Let's break that down:

- Incremental revenue needed is $40m.
- You have a total of 730 days to deliver it
- You have five offices around the world.
- That boils down to $55,000 per day globally
- Spread among five offices that's $11,000 per day per office.

That concentrates the mind. How does that feel? Does it feel attainable? What's your current run rate for new revenue per office per day? Whatever the difference is between your run rate and your target rate is the scale of the task. We can pretty much guess that you won't be putting on business – let alone incremental business – at the rate of $55,000 per day. Therefore, something has to change.

That something is the way you attract and go after new business.

This exercise forces our clients to evaluate their new business systems and practices from scratch and in a very cold-hearted way, to redesign the shop window so it attracts attention. We have to be honest with ourselves when we are faced with a concrete financial task from which there is no escape. A demanding shareholder permits no escape. We have to re-evaluate everything and this starts with looking at the barriers which get in the way of doing business development better.

The usual barriers are:

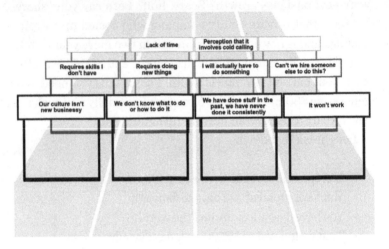

1. Lack of time – I am too busy working on important existing client business.
2. Perception that it entails cold calling . . . which, in turn, entails discomfort, flogging our wares shamelessly and behaving in a way that doesn't sit well with our company culture or my own personal ethics.
3. Requires new skills I don't have.
4. Requires doing new things I don't particularly like doing or can't be bothered to learn.
5. I will actually have to do something, and the effect will be visible and measurable, and I will be held to account.

6. Can't we hire someone to do this?
7. Our culture isn't new businessy.
8. We don't know what to do or how to do it.
9. We have done stuff in the past but we have never done it consistently.
10. It won't work.

There is an answer to each and every one of these barriers that people erect. Before we give our version of an answer, try running a workshop with your senior team to break down your own financial target into an amount of extra money per day that's needed and create your own list of barriers that will get in the way of achieving this sum. Then generate some answers that get you all over these barriers.

Here's our solution to getting over the barriers:

1. Lack of time – too busy working on important existing client business

Of course you are. So is everyone else. Everyone in any business is always too busy with the urgent to do the important. But we all agree new business is very important and is now our number-one priority, yes? If it isn't yet, it will be urgent very soon by necessity. So we need to look at how we carve our time availability differently. That requires flexibility and self-discipline. What if you all agreed to free up 20 per cent of your week to devote to new business development? How do you do this? Well, if you look at how Google operate, every single employee is entitled to 20 per cent of their week (one day in five) to devote to a personal project they feel passionate about. If a company as fast-growing and busy as Google is able to free up 20 per cent of their employees' time to do this, why is it beyond your team to do the same on a priority objective?

Also, we tend to focus on where we direct our attention. There needs to be a focus on new business – that requires deprioritisation of other areas. So look at your calendars and properly evaluate where that time can either be taken from or where that time can be offloaded on to your colleagues to free you up to work on new business. Most people can free up between 5 per cent and 25 per cent of their time simply by eliminating that low-brain engagement work (such as email responses, unnecessary meetings, social media distraction) that eats up so much time of the day. If you schedule 'deep work' – work that requires concentrated thinking time - into your day when your natural energy levels and creativity are at their peak, and discipline yourself to allocate time for general admin such as emails for when you are just ticking over, you will transform your productivity and quality of output. In other words, don't be a busy fool!

2. Perception that it entails cold calling . . . which, in turn, entails discomfort, flogging our wares shamelessly and behaving in a way that doesn't sit well with our company culture or personal ethics

Oh dear. Here is the great bogeyman of new business: I will have to sell! I will have to pick up the phone and talk to strangers. I will have to prostitute myself and our company by nakedly, ambitiously asking total strangers to give us their business.

Garbage.

Get to know them. Place yourself on their radar. Gently posit that you might have something useful to help their business – at least it's worth a chat.

3. Requires new skills I don't have

All human beings have the essential skills to do new business. The ability to contact an acquaintance either via email or phone or on

Facebook or LinkedIn (or on other social media), point out to them that you haven't seen each other for far too long, and suggest you go for an orange juice, a beer or a coffee soon. Or to contact them and say, 'Our mutual friend, Louisa Clarke, mentioned that you might be interested in meeting because she was talking to you recently about xyz and we've just done some work in that area. Would you like to get together to discuss what we found? Apart from anything else, it's always nice to meet friends of Louisa's!' You do have the skills to do such a simple thing.

4. Requires doing new things I don't particularly like doing or can't be bothered to learn

What's wrong with meeting people? They aren't going to bite. You don't like writing blogs or thought leadership papers? You don't like sharing your knowledge? When did you stop growing as a human being and become so isolationist and stuck in your ways? Doing new things, accepting new challenges, isn't that the way we all grow and develop? Try taking a growth mindset survey and see if you've become atrophied. Since when was it acceptable just to do the things you have always done the way you have always done them, and get rewarded for it?

If you always do what is easy and choose the path of least resistance, you never step out of your comfort zone. Great things never come from comfort zones.

Companies, like people, only grow by evolving, by learning to do new things, learning new skills, changing with the times. We only get transformational results if we transform ourselves and get new skills. Welcome the new things you have to do to generate new business – they will take you in new directions and help you discover things about the world and yourself.

5. I will actually have to do something, and the effect will be visible and measurable, and I will be held to account

Yes, you will! New business is not a forgiving taskmistress. She is a ravenous beast, always hungry for more. But you know what? The more you give the more you will get and the more you get the easier it will be, because effort begets success and success begets more success. Welcome accountability; there is little in business life more rewarding than being able to trace your own footsteps back to being the prime cause of a new client joining your company. It is something worth celebrating. Why hide your light under a bushel? If you and your organisation are as good as you believe at helping clients, surely more clients deserve to benefit from your skills? Yes, you will have to devote time to reconnecting with old contacts, and nurturing them, and listening out for when they might actually benefit from a conversation with you about work, but isn't that time well spent?

Yes, you will have to do something. You will have to take action. And you will have to take action deliberately and consistently – no 'stop-start' for you anymore. Yes, you will have to be self-disciplined. Yes, you will not be forgiven for excuses like, 'Well, I met a few old contacts last month, but I haven't done anything this month.' Once you start, you cannot stop. But that's OK. It will become addictive because you will, believe it or not, start to enjoy it. You will enjoy it because you will be staying in touch with people you probably like, and the more you get to know them and their needs, the less likely it will be that you will feel you are 'flogging' stuff to them that they don't want. You are just staying in touch until they might need your expertise, and when they do, you will be there, ready, waiting and willing to help.

Doesn't sound so bad, now, does it?

6. Can't we hire someone to do this?

No. You can't. You can hire someone to make sure you do it and to help you do it. But these are *your* personal contacts – those you have collected in your business career, or those your friends and colleagues have passed on to you, when you asked them if there was anyone they knew in business that they would be happy to refer to you. This is something you must do, part of your contract to help the organisation you love and have pride in and that pays your salary, to grow and thrive.

Yes, every good new business organisation harnesses the talent it has to harvest the contacts each of their people have. But you don't have to do it alone. You can go see your contacts with a colleague (remember, hunting in pairs is good) and introduce them over a coffee; you can co-author a blog or a think piece; you can attend an industry conference or event one evening with a couple of your workmates. New business doesn't have to be a lonesome activity. In fact, it is much more effective when it is a collective endeavour.

7. Our culture isn't new businessy

It is now. If your idea of a new business culture is synonymous with it being crass, venal, obvious, harassing of clients, relentlessly cold-calling – well, then, you have the wrong image in your head. But we have never seen a business that was proud of what it did that didn't also want to help more clients do things better or more effectively. That's all new business is: putting yourself and your organisation in the way of helping more people and client organisations to do stuff better. What's not to like?

8. We don't know what to do or how to do it

Er, read this book and then, even more importantly, do what we suggest.

9. We have done stuff in the past but we have never done it consistently

Classic. Well, spoiler alert, maybe that's why it hasn't worked. All of the stuff that we are talking about works. It all works without fail. We know this because we do it all the time and we win lots of new clients. But the secret to success is that you do it relentlessly, every day, day in and day out. There is no let up. There are no off days. You do it systematically, methodically and with vigour and energy. And you keep going. You keep going until you get the contact. You keep going until you get the meeting. You keep going until you get the next meeting. And the next. You stay in touch until you hear them say, 'Do you know anyone who can help us with . . .', and then, if you cannot help them, you do your best to put them in touch (personally introduce) with someone you know who *can* help them. And if that person is you, well, lovely.

If you do all this consistently, it then becomes a case of simple mathematics:

- Fifteen senior people connecting with two people per week that they have lost touch with, or get referred to, or meet at an event, etc.
- (15 people x 2 client contacts each week) x 52 weeks) x 5 offices = 7,800 new contacts for your company. In two years that's 15,600 contacts in your new business pipeline.
- At a 2 per cent conversion rate that's 312 new clients.
- At $30,000 per client that's $9,360,000 incremental

revenue for the price of 15,600 coffees (roughly $46,800 at $3 per coffee).

- You're on your way to pleasing the shareholder and making your target.
- At a 10 per cent conversion rate you will increase incremental revenue by $46,800,000, exceeding your target.

10. It won't work

No, it won't. Not if you carry that attitude with you everywhere. For something to change, someone has to change. But people hate change. They loathe it. Hypocritically, they replay all the platitudes on PowerPoint presentations to clients about how the *only* inevitability in life is change . . . and then they do everything, and we mean everything, in their power to avoid doing anything differently themselves. Well, here's another platitude for you: if you don't make the change happen, then change will happen to you – whether you want it or not. It will. It is better to be in charge of the change in your life than for it to be in charge of you. When it is in charge of you, and you aren't prepared for it or accepting of it, that's when companies become obsolete and people outlive their relevance.

Look around your workplace. Remember Julian? Stalwart of the company. Lovely guy. My, he looked after his clients well. But he never really moved with the times, did he? He got rather stuck in his ways. Became rather a fuddy-duddy. Until, one day, he wasn't needed anymore. Same can be said of Kodak. Or Woolworths, or Borders, or Toys "R" Us, or Compaq, or Blockbuster, or Pan Am, or BHS, or TWA, or Debenhams, or Carluccio's or Flybe. The list goes on.

Adapt, or die.

CHAPTER 10

WHO, WHAT, HOW? GET YOUR STORY STRAIGHT

'Luke, you're going to find that many of the truths we
cling to depend greatly on our own point of view'
Obi-Wan Kenobi, *Star Wars: Episode VI Return of the Jedi*

We're not big fans of process and spreadsheets. It's our belief that one of the biggest hindrances to new business success can be 'busywork' – work that occupies a disproportionate amount of time but yields zero results. That said, we do believe that there are some areas where it is worth investing your time, and 'getting your story straight' is one of them.

Your business is a brand. It may not be a famous brand or one with a big marketing spend and a range of merchandise, but it is a brand. And brands are valuable assets for businesses.

This is true for businesses that sell directly to consumers, and also for B2B organisations for whom reputation matters. Put simply, if you can't explain clearly what you're selling, how can you expect people to buy it?

When we work with big corporates, we'll often have up to twelve people in a room and ask them to tell us what the company they work for does. Nine times out of ten we get twelve different explanations. Does it matter, though? Surely, we shouldn't all be robots, trotting out the same lines on repeat? Agreed, no one wants to be on the end of what we call 'Brochurey' – a language familiar to those in professional services which sounds like the corporate brochure being read out, industry jargon and all. But, consistency in terms of the messaging of who you are, what you do and how you do it (that makes you different from your competition) is important. A bit of upfront work here saves you time in the long run. Like it or not, we're all brand ambassadors. How we behave both in and out of work sends a strong message to external audiences. If those messages are both positive and consistent, we increase our share of voice versus our competitors so that potential clients, recruits and the media are better aware of our offer and capabilities. Better awareness means more opportunities for client approaches, being first choice for recruitment and a strong story to tell within the media. In an article on Forbes.com, Rieva Lesonsky points out that strong brands are critical for B2B success: 'When shopping for vendors and solutions, they [B2B buyers] look at peer recommendations and review sites (65%) and social media (54%) more than they used to.'[*] Like consumers, professional buyers use the vendor's reputation as a shortcut which reduces risk and simplifies the evaluation process

Let's turn to the CIA to guide our approach. Allegedly, the CIA has an expression: 'Know what you need to know before you believe what you want to believe.' It's a good one to keep in mind if you're worried about your company's performance with clients and potential clients. Too often we screen out unwelcome feedback and more often clients don't even want to give it to us. But if your pipeline is worryingly sparse, if you're not converting the leads you do get or you're failing to grow your

---

[*] Rieva Lesonsky, 'What Does it Take to Sell to the New B2B Buyer?', Forbes. com (May, 2019).

existing clients, it's vital to find out what's not working, as well as confirming what you're doing well.

How can you find this information out? Ask them. Talk to your current and potential clients. Talk to those who have chosen not to work with you as well. So often we make assumptions about why a client is behaving in a particular way or what they may be thinking about us (if they are thinking about us at all). The only way to find out for sure is to ask them.

If you feel awkward about picking up the phone and asking your client for the brutal truth about you, bring in a third party to help. Most clients are decent people who want to be liked. They may tell you what they think you want to hear rather than the unvarnished truth, which, whilst it may be painful to hear, is most valuable to you. In our experience we have found that people are willing to help with honest feedback, and that they respect the organisation more for seeking it.

Arrange a maximum of six one-on-one interviews with clients who have bought from you and some of the prospect pitches you lost or meetings that didn't progress. You don't need lots of data; you do need informed opinion that is brutally frank.

It's also critical to get your own input and personal perspectives of your understanding of the past and your ambitions for the future. If there are other key people in the organisation whose perspective would be useful, invite them to do the same.

Questions to ask your clients and prospects:

- What three words would you use to describe our company?
- Which companies do you think are our competitors?
- What three words would you use to describe them?
- What should we do better?

- How would you describe our people?
- How would you rate your interaction with us?
- What makes us different?
- What do you want from us that you're not getting currently?
- What was it that made the difference when you awarded the business to us/the competitor?

Questions to ask yourself:

- Why did you set up the company? Or, what attracted you to join the company?
- How would you describe your ideal target client? (Try to describe them attitudinally rather than by job title or industry sector)
- What is your proposition in the market? (The single most important thing you can say about your brand, product or service)
- How would you describe your positioning in the market? (How you want to be perceived relative to your competitors)
- If you only had three words or phrases to describe the company at its best, what would they be?
- What new areas should we be investing in to ensure we don't, in the words of Silicon Valley companies, 'miss the future'?

These external and internal interviews will give you key insights and perspectives to ensure that the positioning work that is your next task is as effective as possible. They will help to drive concise and clear answers to the most important questions in business development:

- Who should we be selling to?
- What should we offer them?
- Why should they buy from us and no one else?

We've explained earlier that we don't want to be restrictive when it comes to identifying your target client; new business can come from anywhere. However, it is useful to agree on an attitudinal target (how they behave) rather than a demographic target (a particular sector or type) so that you can spot a 'fellow traveller' that may be more receptive to your charms. For example, our target client is what we call 'impatient leaders' – senior people who are in a hurry to grow their business and brand or who want personal growth by developing their leadership effectiveness.

A company specialising in advising on mergers and acquisitions had a similar senior target audience but articulated it in a way that was specific to them. Their target audience was 'leaders looking for leaders' – leading companies who are ready for a deal and who want, need and value smart direction from a trusted advisor who will deliver the best deal in their best interests.

The tell and sell

Once you've clearly identified the client most likely to buy from you, and obtained the answers to your questions from your clients and prospects, and also from the key people within your organisation, you are on your way to creating a 'tell' and a 'sell' for your company.

The 'tell' answers the question, 'If your company or brand or service didn't exist, why would you create it?' It starts with your purpose and your proposition (having identified your target client).

The 'sell' is what you do, how you do it and why you do it – the things that make you different.

To help you populate your 'tell and sell', ask yourself (and, of course, answer) these questions:

- How do we behave that sets us apart from our competition?
- Why should people believe us?
- What's different and special about the people who work for us?
- What are the hallmarks of the way we treat our clients?
- What is our tone of voice when we communicate?

This identifies where you are now. But if you don't like the answers, try taking a more future-focused approach. These questions are less about finding out what the current situation is, and more about identifying a vision of your firm in the future. Once you know where you're aiming, you can create a plan to get there.

- What do we want to be famous for?
- What should distinguish how we behave as an organisation?
- What are the specific things we'll do that will give reasons to believe us?
- What should characterise the people who work for us?
- What should be the hallmark of the way we treat our clients?
- What should consistently characterise our tone of voice/ communications?

We're not looking for reams of paper here but the answers to these questions should help clarify the why, what and how of your business: why you exist, what you offer and how you do it. And once you are clear on that, build up your bank of stories and examples to prove the point that will make it easy for you to tell your story and demonstrate why you are best placed to help clients.

When you articulate your offer, make sure it's differentiating; it's better to be a strong flavour that polarises opinion than to be bland and disappear. If you try to please everyone, you will end up appealing to no one. And don't try to explain everything you do. Prioritise. Focus on the best thing you do. Why? Because of the 'distinction paradox'* If you claim to be the world's greatest expert at X, clients will probably ask if you can do Y and Z as well. (You can). But if you claim to do all three upfront, no one will ask you to do any of them. Specific expertise is believable and hooks clients in. So concentrate and dominate. And remember: once you've proven yourself in this specific area, it will be a cinch to migrate the client to other services you provide.

* Andy Cowles and Andy Pemberton. Furthr.co.uk

CHAPTER 11

CREATING AN IRRESISTIBLE SHOP WINDOW

'I will go to my grave believing that participation is
best driven by the well-stocked shop window'
Sebastian Coe

We work with a lot of companies who have steep new business acquisition targets. Normally these stringent targets are the result of a combination of factors:

- Jittery management suddenly panicking that all their eggs are in too few client baskets so a sales push is required;
- The need to recover their trading position post-economic shutdown due to COVID-19;
- Shareholders who require ambitious growth from their investment prior to a sale of the business;
- An earnout that looks in jeopardy as the profitability and top-line growth figures start to indicate that the financial windfall for the principals might be in jeopardy;
- A change of CEO who understands that the quickest and most effective route back to the top of the league table in their industry is to have a string of high-profile new business wins – it acts as a magnet for talent to join the organisation and nothing is more irresistible to clients than other clients flocking to a 'hot' advisory company.

We also tend to work with companies who are extremely good at their technical competence and skill set. Law firms who are outstanding legal eagles; accountants who are sharp as a knife; architects who build iconic structures; management consultancies who save their clients millions; investment banks who have a Soros-style eye for a deal; insurance firms who manage risk, beautifully; communication agencies who increase their clients' sales with clever publicity. All these companies exhibit genius in their chosen field of competence.

And yet they are consistently outshone in new business acquisition by less technically competent competitors. Why? Because the less technically competent compensate for their inferior product by creating a shopfront window that is irresistible.

Second-rate practitioners tend to their own image assiduously. They slave over their website and Twitter feed, and are always in the trade and national media, because they know that this increases their reputation within their target community. They are high-profile and loud – they stick their heads above the parapet because it pays for them to do so. In the absence of technical heft and intellectual brilliance, they substitute visibility and bedazzling sparkle. They exude energy and dynamism and this impresses new business prospects.

Energy and dynamism are extremely attractive. What client doesn't want energy and dynamism from their strategic partners?

This aura of excitement is very seductive and these companies turn it into new business success. They are serial networkers, masters at the art of seduction. But even though their image is veneer-thin, it is sufficient to seduce enough prospects into their new business pipeline to generate a continuous supply of wins. Wins which they merchandise ruthlessly, thereby enhancing their own reputation even further.

Having a sexy shop window is a crucial component of new business attractiveness. It is the package which entices people in. Just look at how much attention the world's top retailers (both physical and virtual) pay to their shopfront window displays – Amazon, ASOS, Farfetch, Selfridges, Harvey Nichols, Galeries Lafayette, Gucci, Ralph Lauren. They don't do it for fun.

But so many of the technically brilliant companies we work with pay scant, if any, attention to their own shop window. (They are usually too busy working on their clients' business.) It is tired and sad and doesn't work for them the way it could. While they make their clients shine, their own website, thought leadership, marketing and reputation management are dull and lacklustre. Their outbound new business effort is sporadic and generic, shambolic or, worst of all, non-existent. Their own shopfront window is moribund. It lacks glamour, is opaque in explaining what they do, has out-of-date information, redundant testimonials and obsolete case studies. Their case studies are badly written and poorly organised. The biographies are off the shelf, amateur and dull. Nothing about their face to the world is compelling or exciting.

It is like walking past the virtual equivalent of those old-fashioned clothing shops in country towns where the whole window is swathed in yellow cellophane to stop the clothes in the window bleaching in the daylight. They look ancient and behind the times. They do no justice to the brilliance inside the organisation.

So many companies are utterly inattentive to their environment and the mood they create in the mind of the new business prospect – whether the impression is made virtually with their website and online presence, or in the reception area of their office and meeting rooms. You can almost feel the cobwebs settling on the organisation, the tumbleweed rolling down the corridors.

We have worked with a digital agency who offer 'word of mouth' marketing to their clients, but who generate zero word of mouth among the client community about their agency. It's not that they're no good at what they do – they have a client list to die for – it's just that they are so busy attending to their clients' needs that they have forgotten to attend to their own. Their biggest competitor is a company run by a man called Hank Veeker (names have been changed to protect the innocent, but these are real companies and real people). Hank doesn't forget to merchandise himself and his company; in fact, he is a genius at it. He has a very impressive profile on Wikipedia. It reads like the biography of Aristotle Onassis, and mentions his numerous philanthropic causes, his personal net worth and his life back-story. He is on the cover of every trade magazine and website and is always being quoted in the media. He is rent-a-quote. Who do you think is more top of mind in the client community? You know the answer. Who is technically better at what they specialise in? Again, you know the answer.

It might be a sad reflection of the world we live in that the reputational plaudits go not necessarily to the best performers but to the *most attractive and noisiest* performers. You may not like it, but you need to play, however vulgar you might think it is.

Because the days of 'if we build it, they will come' are long gone. Time was that the world worked in such a way that when you did good work, people noticed and came to see what you could do for them. Not anymore. The world is too busy and noisy now, with way more competition in every field of endeavour. The world changes and the rules move on. If you don't play by those rules, well, you better be the world's best and there is precious little room for many of them. For everyone else, you need to be a bit vulgar – you need to get out there. You need to have a shop window that attracts new customers to your door.

'The aura given out by a person or object is as much a part of them as their flesh' Lucien Freud

It's all about positioning. It's all about creating an aura around yourself and your organisation. It's all about the comparisons you make and the company you put yourself alongside. People want to work with companies and individuals who look and feel like they are winning, making noise, moving and shaking.

Burnishing your public image is a full-time and unrelenting job. It is the essence of being credible and open for business. If the product or service you supply behind the shopfront window is world class, so much the better. But many companies thrive on simply attracting enough people through the front door because they are dazzled by the shopfront display.

When we set up our company, we were extremely mindful of the need to create a shop window for ourselves which gave our company the aura of success, dynamism, intellectual heft, influence and gravitas way beyond our status as a start-up. Everything we did added cumulatively to the impression of being a serious contender in the world of consultancy. From the off, we published books – two about winning pitches and winning more business from existing clients. One about the need to be bold in business, another on the need to create purpose in your enterprise and another about how to lead at speed. We negotiated a regular column in the British Airways *Business Life* magazine – a very high-profile shop window which really got noticed and lent us a stature way in advance of our revenue. We held a party every January (Christmas being a waste of time because clients are inundated with invitations and are exhausted by the end of December but who welcome the oasis of a party in the doldrums of January) and every summer, regardless of our financial fortunes. Guests – even those who can't attend but get the invitation – fill in the gap that things are good in your world. Nothing sells success like the confidence to hold a party, especially in the midst of a financial crisis. We ran regular think-ins, hosting eminent speakers with new books out or on interesting subjects and important issues either in select dinners or at breakfast debates. We opened offices in Singapore and New York City. We persuaded a well-known, eminent business leader to be our company chairman. We held our strategic planning sessions in New York, Singapore, Valencia, Lisbon and Jersey – and we told anyone and everyone we did this because, again, people fill in the blanks.

To be honest, it costs very little more (and sometimes less) to hold a three-day meeting abroad than it does to hold it in the UK. But the signal it sends externally, and the positive effect on morale internally, more than compensate. It gives you something to say. It gives another piece of evidence that your firm is prospering and is a player on the international stage, and that working for it or with it gives you a different experience.

Additionally, we took photos of all our client gigs, parties and strategic meetings overseas and published them on our website (with permission of course). We were active in social media, producing a blog every week and merchandising these via Facebook, LinkedIn and Twitter. They often got picked up by other media and republished.

We focused wholeheartedly on our shopfront window – it is as much a part of catalysing new relationships as a face-to-face meeting. Especially in this era of Zoom communications and maintaining a presence across multiple platforms.

Show off

A few years ago, the *Guardian* newspaper ran an open weekend at their offices in the King's Cross area of London. This was a distinctively on-brand event, tailored to the loyal and participative readership that this national newspaper cultivates, for whom it was essential to attend. The event was immersive, grand, exciting; with lectures, workshops, seminars and discussion groups alongside artists, journalists, economists, celebrities, actors, authors, cartoonists and commentators on culture, the arts, business, politics – you name it. There were *Guardian* masterclasses on podcasting, building websites, writing your novel. There were interviews with artists such as Grayson Perry. There were poetry readings. The weekend was two extraordinary days of intellectual and sensory stimulation. At a time when the newspaper was pioneering free-to-access content online, when all other Fleet Street publications were putting up paywalls and introducing subscription services, this single event engendered massive loyalty and a feeling among the participants of being part of a movement, part of the national debate and part of a collective of like-minded individuals. As a shopfront window to re-establish the *Guardian* at the forefront of its readers' lives, it was an unforgettable experience. The effects remain long, long after the event ended.

Similarly, the WPP Group, a leading organisation in the digital communications and publicity sector, runs a three-day immersive event called Stream, which they describe as an '*un*-conference for unconventional people'. Around four hundred invitation-only attendees from the worlds of business, culture, media, entertainment and government – all of whom are united by an interest in all things digital – are brought together at an ex-Club Med hotel in Marathon, Greece, in October (at the end of the summer season so costs are kept under control). WPP pays for the whole event through sponsors, so the venue, food, drink and administration are covered. The participants pay only for their flight to and from Athens.

But you have to sing for your supper. Because it is an un-conference, the content is created entirely by the participants. It is like a free-forming festival of ideas. When you arrive, you put the subject you want to discuss, your name, where you will be and when up on the enormous whiteboards in reception and everyone chooses what they want to attend and take part in. The subjects can be about anything – it is a meritocracy. Some subjects attract loads of people; some just a select few. The idea is to promote dialogue and discussion about issues that matter in the world. Examples from the one we attended include 'How can the digital community help identify people likely to commit either domestic crime or terrorist activities by mapping social media behaviour?', through to 'How the work environment is changing' to 'What does the city of the future look like?'

We would have no doubt that many friends are made here and many conversations begin which end in work and revenue for WPP – and, crucially, for lots of other companies who attend. Remember, seek to help others and you will help yourself. Stream is creative, differentiated and clever. It leverages the power of a holding company to benefit many of its subsidiaries by providing a low-pressure environment in which to network and in which to make friends and influence people. It is also a *must-attend* event for many of the big media and client players in the world. In this way, Stream is a very effective shopfront window for WPP.

Aside from how you behave to fill your shopfront window, there are other weapons at your disposal which can help burnish your image and personality in the marketplace. Two very powerful weapons are how you speak to the world and how you behave in it.

By 'speak', we mean both the verbal and the written communication you deliver. When we started our consultancy, our core promise was to *stimulate*. That became a *cri de coeur* for all our communication, whether it was a book, a speech, a blog, a proposal, a phone call or even just an email.

It isn't enough, if your mission is to stimulate, to write a bog-standard proposal. The proposal has to be brilliant – engaging, compelling and superbly reasoned. It has to be perfectly presented and delivered with due ceremony and in a memorable way. To help our new recruits understand how we communicate, we taught them how to do it our way. We produced booklets that explained and showed examples of how to speak and write our particular stimulating language fluently. And we produced stories about what we had created for our clients, how we had approached the task and delivered results. These were straight-talking, written in the vernacular and designed to engage the reader with a super-honest story about what we had done and how we had done it. These stories were so much more than the dry, dead case studies that most companies write. They were vital, authentic and had a tone of voice which burnished our reputation for doing things in our own inimitable style.

We also *behaved* differently. We created a code of behaviour which ran through all our interactions both internal and external:

- **We behaved with 'heart and conscience'** – we would always seek to do the right thing. We always want to do the right thing by ourselves and also by our clients. We want to work with all effort and ethically.
- **We promised clients we would be 'respectfully disrespectful'** – we would tell them what we thought regardless of whether it was politic or polite to say it. We wouldn't do this gracelessly, but we wouldn't shirk our responsibility to be an honest counsellor.
- **We promised we would act 'in a hurry but never in a rush'** – we would always move at speed but never compromise the quality of the task.

All of these values helped us to signal to our clients and our community that we are a particular sort of consultancy. That they could expect only straight-talking from us, and that we saw our role to challenge not to acquiesce or chase our own interest. We reasoned that people would pay us for our thoughtful opinion, and that the moment we went native in a client's organisation, we would cease to be of value to them. Our whole offer is about being the outsider looking in.

We also set out to become 'the consultants' consultant', a vanity we reasoned would speak volumes about the regard we were held in if we could claim that the world's best consultancy firms looked to us when they needed help to grow or to present a better shopfront window to the world. Your client list is often one of the most potent symbols you can have to signal you are a serious contender, and we assiduously collected client names and testimonials to post on our site. At one stage we were able to describe ourselves as working with the fastest growing auto company in Europe, the fastest growing fashion brand in the world, the world's biggest real estate company and the world's top advertising agency group new business winner. We masterminded our accountancy client winning the biggest domestic pitch in the UK that year, our global advertising agency client winning the largest international pitch in the same year and our real estate client of the time winning the biggest property pitch in their market.

In total, we were instrumental in helping our clients add $1 billion of incremental revenue within just three years of opening our doors. We won the accolade of the UK's best growth agency in the first awards held for this sector five years later, demonstrating a consistency of performance that made us the go-to experts for new business development growth. Although we haven't yet become the 'consultants' consultant', we have clients in every field of professional services consultancy except architecture and management consultancy. Nearly there.

Manufacture how you wish to be perceived

In many industries there are various surveys, awards and league tables which, if exploited properly, provide additional 'reasons to believe'. These are stories that burnish your reputation and make your shopfront window sparkle even brighter. Opinion is divided on whether these are always worth entering or chasing. However, if you judiciously pick the single most influential award or survey to focus on winning, it just gives you more to shout about and helps perpetuate the impression that you are at the top of your game. This is an important impression to create because clients want to work with successful partner companies, as we have already stated.

If your reception area has a glass cabinet with trophies awarded a decade ago that have lost their sheen both literally and metaphorically, then you can be sure that although you and your colleagues have become blind to their presence (and what it says about your organisation), new clients and even existing clients definitely do notice. What this display of bygone glory days says is that you are off the pace. No longer sexy. Beware the impression you are unwittingly creating because if you aren't doing it thoughtfully, you are thoughtlessly implanting a negative image in the mind of your prospective clients. Oh, and your existing clients will start to be susceptible to the overtures of sexier competitors who have polished cabinets gleaming with recently won awards and who, you can be sure, are in touch with them and offering help.

Your shopfront window is too important to leave to chance. It needs to sparkle and dazzle. So do you. If you can make the industry league tables and client surveys work to your advantage then do so – if you don't, your competitors will.

In new business, *everything* matters – absolutely everything. Every detail. You must obsess about every single detail of your shopfront window. Nothing is too small to merit your attention.

CHAPTER 12

IN THE BEGINNING WAS THE WORD: MAKING YOUR MESSAGE SHINE

'The thing about hip hop today is it's smart, it's
insightful. The way they can communicate a complex
message in a very short space is remarkable'
Barack Obama

No company can afford to waste assets – especially when many
firms are in a race for survival during the worst economic situation in modern history. The utilisation of assets is a vital
financial discipline for businesses. Words are assets – both
spoken and written. In every business on planet Earth, words
are our primary tools to persuade, cajole, propose and prove in
order to make more profit. Whatever business we are in, be it
construction or client service, we all need to make our written
and spoken words work harder for their living. Today, more
than ever before, we all need to sweat these assets harder.

In business, we use words to get results. Too often, the words
we write generate bad results or even no result. Too much
communication – both written and spoken – is verbose,
unedited, badly phrased, leaden, uninteresting, grammatically
incorrect, grandiose, hyperbolic and unpersuasive. This is
especially true in written communication where corporate
puffery is rife. But it is also true in our spoken word and

presentations. The amount of unrehearsed presentations taking place on planet Earth on any given working day is tragic. Microsoft calculated that there are approximately thirty million presentations given every day. In the vast majority of these, the presenter will be sending the audience to sleep and wasting valuable time being bad at communicating. We think this is criminal.

In this vital area, we turn to the ancients for advice, most notably, Aristotle. In *Rhetoric*, Aristotle identified the five components of persuasive communication: Ethos (character or credibility), Logos (reason), Pathos (emotion) plus metaphor and brevity. It is comforting to know that nothing has changed in the intervening two thousand plus years since he wrote this definitive guide.

Carmine Gallo is a Harvard University instructor in the department of Executive Education at the Graduate School of Design. He analysed the top 500 most popular TED Talks of all time and found there was a common pattern to the content: on average, 65 per cent of the talks were focused on stories (Pathos), 25 per cent on Logos (logic) and only 10 per cent on Ethos (your authority as an expert or your credentials).[*] All the most successful Ted Talks are primarily made up of stories. Gallo quotes TED curator, Chris Anderson: 'The stories that can generate the best connection are stories about you personally or about people close to you. Tales of failure, awkwardness, misfortune, danger or disaster, told authentically, hastens deep engagement.' People respond to how you make them *feel* and are prompted to action by the personal connection you establish with them as a result. The best way to establish rapport with others is through storytelling, and his observation is borne

[*] Carmine Gallo, 'The Art of Persuasion Hasn't Changed in 2,000 Years', *Harvard Business Review* (July 2019).

out by twenty-first century neuroscience – stories trigger a rush of chemicals to the brain, including, most importantly, oxytocin, which is the drug that connects people, creating empathy and trust between them.

To gauge how effective your communication is at driving connection with your audience, measure the relative percentage of your presentation or document devoted to your credentials (Ethos), facts and the logic of your case (Logos) and storytelling (Pathos). We suspect you'll find that Pathos is low and the other two make up a disproportionately large part of the whole. Oh dear. Instead, ensure all your written communication is sharp, correct, pithy, vital and to the point. It should contain personal insight and stories in order to connect with the audience. If it has these things, you will differentiate yourself and your organisation from the herd immediately. You will be a beacon of excellence in a sea of sameness and conformity. Do this in both your spoken and written work. But especially your written work, which is all too often dry and lacking in personality. Why? Because now, more than ever before, business is conducted in the written word. Email, texting, messaging, documents, pitch books, RFIs and RFPs, presentations, thought pieces, proposals, reports, appraisals – the list goes on. We are drowning in the written word.

Not only is there more competition for your reader's attention, but they are also increasingly reading all these words in formats which constantly distract and promote skim reading. Hyperlinks in articles take your reader off in other directions; reading on a mobile device has created new, compressed writing formats – which is a shame because most people's business writing is anything but compressed. And people have got used to reading everything on the go in a frantically noisy world where their attention is also being distracted by video, podcasts and a host of other intrusive media.

The onus is on you to make your words and your organisation's communications work very hard for their living – both when you speak them and set them down on screen or on paper. In your organisation, every employee should understand the need to treat the company's word assets just the same as they would treat its other valuable assets, such as its customers: considerately and with respect.

Credentials documents and presentations

We hate credentials. Clients hate credentials. They are a substitute for focusing the conversation on what really matters: the prospect's business. However, we understand the need to organise your story so that the key elements are in one place. It's also useful to have everything at hand for intermediaries and for when you have to create bid submission documents.

First meetings often include a request to share credentials – what you do, how you do it, what makes you different. There are three types of credentials presentations:

1. Thirty-second 'elevator pitch': We often talk about having an 'elevator pitch' prepared and ready. You never know when someone will ask you what you do or what your company does. If you spurt out a load of incomprehensible, jargon-laden drivel, you will not only lose your audience but you have also lost an opportunity. If you are a fisherman or a farmer, it's easy. If, however, you work in a role that cannot be described by the function you fulfil but which requires considerable elaboration, or where the benefit of what you do isn't immediately discernible, then you need to work on your elevator pitch.

It should be as simple as you can possibly make it – so simple your granny can understand it. It needs to be this simple because if it isn't, whoever you are talking to won't remember it; they will only remember the impression you leave them with, which will be that you do something that sounds overblown, pretentious and incomprehensible. If it's too simple – 'I'm a banker', for example – they will fill in the gap with all the images they have built up over the years of what a banker is and does. This may not necessarily be flattering or do justice to your particular facet of banking. Quite often, using an analogy can be helpful.

> You know those amazing mechanics who fine-tune Formula 1 racing car engines to extract the maximum performance out of them for the race? Well, we are like those mechanics, only we fine-tune the components of your sales process/supply chain/front of house/marketing spend/production line/ financial operations/property investments/team dynamics/ assets/digital communications, etc., so they run at maximum efficiency and better than those of your competitors.

An elevator pitch is useful because, apart from anything else, it should remind you of what it is you actually do. We know several companies that take this seriously and have an agreed elevator pitch which is shared with all employees.

A company we know, the market leader in the area of shopper marketing, describe what they do with this simple explanation: 'If your product isn't there, it can't be bought. We make sure it's there, wherever and whenever people want to buy it.'

At our consultancy we describe ourselves by virtue of the sort of clients we work with: 'We help impatient leaders grow their business, brands and people faster than they could on their own.'

Perhaps the best-known elevator pitch was the one given to a journalist by the guy sweeping the floor of the hangar where the *Apollo 11* rocket was being assembled. When asked, 'What's your job?', he replied: 'I'm sending a man to the moon.'

2. Two to five minutes – first meeting: Again, you need to be clear and concise here – the purpose is to outline your credibility by covering your positioning statement, what makes you different (don't just say, 'our people') and your unique areas of expertise. Make it a well-rehearsed, interesting, engaging and fluent tour de force – a few judicious facts and statistics leavened with an illustrative anecdote and a pithy quotation. But do it all in two minutes.

Think about the audience. Think about the four major behavioural styles. If they are Analyticals, go in heavy on the facts. If they are Expressives, up the ante on the storytelling. If they are Amiables, talk about your team and theirs. If they are Drivers, focus on the results. If they are some combination of all of them, give something for everyone. Resist the temptation to churn through a series of case studies. As one of our clients once said, 'The trouble with companies sharing past work is that it's like sharing pictures of your children: lovely, but I don't care.' You want the majority of the meeting to be spent asking the prospect questions, not talking about yourself.

3. *Ten-minutes plus:* A credentials presentation of this length should only take place for larger meetings, if they have asked for it and if you are weaving in specific responses to how what you do can clearly benefit the client.

You need to be a brilliant presenter, otherwise that ten minutes is going to be the longest in everyone's life as you plough on and on, 'We do this . . . and we also do this . . .' Kill me now.

If you do have a ten-minutes plus credentials meeting in the diary, this agenda is designed to make the meeting valuable for both parties:

- What you (the prospect) said you wanted to cover. This is to force the meeting host to have contacted the prospect in advance to establish what issues are important and relevant to cover in the meeting (and to force the prospect to invest their interest in the meeting rather than just politeness or vague commitment).

- What we have done to prepare for today's meeting (to force yourself to conduct research into the business issues the client is facing and where you can help best).
- What experience we have in your sector/with your issues.
- What three key issues are facing the prospect (to force you to have a point of view).
- The consequences for your business if these issues go unaddressed (to create a commercial imperative for the client to act and to put, where possible, a price on inaction).
- How you believe you can help and a (gentle) suggested next action (to force a trial close and to generate a next meeting).

What does success look like?

What do you want them to *feel, think* and *do* as a result of meeting you? It is an essential discipline in preparing for a meeting to be as intentional as you can about the desired outcome. Agreeing the answers to these three questions helps you know where you are aiming.

The feeling they will take away with them about you is vitally important because people shorthand their experiences and remember the feelings you created inside them: elated; optimistic; concerned. Think hard about what emotion you want to stir in your audience.

Similarly, what do you want them to think about you? *Wow! These guys are really bright*, would be good, wouldn't it? What, specifically, will you say or demonstrate that will make them think this about you?

And finally, all the meetings in the world are useless if nothing happens as a result of them happening. What do you want the audience to *do*? What action do you need them to take? Be specific. And, crucially, ask them to take it. Sounds dumb, doesn't it? But you'd be amazed how many meetings hover at the end in the 'Well, it was nice to meet you' dead zone of zero commitment. Why? Because people are shy to ask or stipulate the next move. Now's the time to wheel out the appropriate closing technique we discussed in Chapter 7 (p.68).

When we're interested in something, our body language changes. We lean forward, use more eye contact and start asking more questions. It's the same for new business meetings. Be alert for questions that are future-focused: 'How would it work? What are the next steps?' – the prospect is showing interest. But be aware: interest doesn't always lead to a sale.

Often you'll be asked for a proposal at the end of a meeting. We usually leap at this invitation as if it is a very positive sign. It is not always a good sign. It can be a means to get rid of you in a way that softens the blow and makes you feel better, or to simply buy time. If they say, 'Send it to me,' it's not necessarily positive.

You can check out the seriousness of the prospect by:

- Challenging the need for a proposal. Ask them what hasn't been covered in the meeting that they need to know, so you can answer now. Ask them, 'What will a proposal add to your understanding?' Too often we take the request to send a proposal as a great result and get the hell out of there, congratulating ourselves that they really bought what we were saying. Try to close now or at least ask what difference a proposal will make. If they still insist, ask them to be specific about precisely what they want you to cover in the written proposal.
- Proposing you come back to present your proposal rather than emailing it.

- Asking them to come to you for the presentation.
- Asking who else needs to see it (and invite them to the next meeting).

In other words, show some spine.

If they still insist on a proposal, send them a maximum of two pages with your brief situation analysis, recommendation, timings and costs. This will flush out whether they are serious (if they agree with the summary and wish to proceed, you can follow up with a more detailed proposal – but only if it is absolutely necessary).

If they're not serious, they're likely to ignore your emails and calls for a meeting, but at least you haven't wasted huge amounts of time drafting a lengthy document. This technique works well and is one we use all the time. If you are able to write succinctly, clearly and persuasively, the requirement for a secondary detailed proposal goes away as the prospect turns into a client and you start the project instead.

Valium or alarm clock?

The opening of a proposal document can either send the reader to sleep or give them a jolt that impels them to read on.

Here's the Valium version:

Dear Sandrine

Thanks for the time you spent sharing with us the brief for your offsite workshop. It is a project that we feel very excited about as we continue to work successfully with other areas of the business.

Our approach – you would like us to facilitate a half-day interactive workshop session in the morning of 19 July. This session should achieve two distinct objectives:

1. *Deliver clarity and coherence around brand vision and values for the Home of the Future (development and agreement);*

2. *Develop a strong team dynamic using engaging group exercises to not only stimulate thinking but also to help everyone network better.*

ZZZZZZZZZZZ

Here's the alarm clock version:

Sandrine

We want your team to go out into the weekend inspired, excited and, most crucially, tooled-up ready to make the Home of the Future a reality following our half-day session on 19 July. Our style is to provoke, to challenge and to help teams co-create ideas which are practical as well as clever, and we will make every minute of our time together both fun and productive. What follows is an explanation of what to expect on the day and how we will work towards that with you. It isn't a cheap workshop. As a rule of thumb, every minute of our workshop delivery involves an hour to plan it, rehearse it and create the materials, exercises and games we will use to bring the session alive. But your team will talk about it for years afterwards and it will truly kick-start the Home of the Future project.

Make your communication create action – not good intentions.

Case studies versus success stories

You can waste a lot of time on case studies. They can be challenging to write – how do you distil a twelve-month project into a few paragraphs? There can be a temptation to go into lots of detail. Avoid that temptation. Your aim here is to provide a brief overview of the project's challenges and its key objective, demonstrate your approach, and highlight the results (any data you have here to prove your point is gold dust). Is there a narrative to this case study? If not, can you create one? We all respond to stories rather than lists of facts. Encourage your team to take photos throughout the lifecycle of a project so you can use them in the case study. Finally, consider calling them 'success stories' rather than case studies. Much more appealing.

You will also differentiate yourselves from the herd if you write up a couple of failure stories too. Remember the client who always asks companies presenting themselves to him to tell him the story of the greatest failure they had and what they learned from it? Honesty is attractive and admission of failure is a great way to create the chemistry of trust. Especially if you can demonstrate what you learned from the failure.

Testimonials

If you do nothing else, get into the habit of asking your clients for a testimonial at the conclusion of a project. Most are happy to give one, and nothing provides more comfort to a prospect than a positive affirmation from an industry peer – especially to Analytical types. If you feel uncomfortable about asking a client for one, get someone else in your firm to do it. Often, if you contact a client and suggest the wording, they will say, 'Great. Use that.' You've saved them a job and you've got a useful testimonial that outlines exactly what you'd like others to say about you.

White papers

For the government, a White Paper is an authoritative report or guide that informs readers concisely about a complex issue and presents the issuing body's point of view on the matter. In business, a white paper is more recognised as a piece of marketing collateral – a tool used to persuade prospects (and clients, and the media) and to promote a particular viewpoint. If you're an expert in a particular industry or sector, sending out regular white papers containing your insights on topical subjects can position you as that holy grail of influence, the thought leader.

But – and it is a big but – sending your thought leadership stuff in an age when global experts on every subject under the sun are holding forth for free on YouTube or TED Talks means your papers had better be damn good. Assuming they are, to give them added relevance, send them out personally wherever possible, with a covering email that's tailored to the recipient. We find nothing more irritating than to suddenly appear on someone's unsolicited mailing list, giving us yet more reading. Sending it personally might just prevent it being deleted. If you don't personalise your communication (because you think that's inefficient and negates the whole point of e-distribution to blanket mail thousands of people), it will just go in the e-trash or spam folder anyway.

RFI (request for information) and RFP (request for proposal)

The first is designed to get you in the race for an assignment. The latter is a consequence of writing a compelling RFI. If you pass the initial test and the prospect client feels you and your company have a good track record and might have something interesting to offer in response to their specific problem, you will be on the shortlist of a final few companies invited to set out what you recommend as a solution. Writing both these documents is an art form. And yet so many times we see slovenly, lazy, slipshod, off-the-shelf, cut-and-paste RFIs and RFPs.

We put this down to the fact that, apparently, so many people don't seem to be able to string a sentence together. Oh, and the fact that these documents are always produced under huge time pressure. Because time is tight, all too often the authors try to save time by borrowing whole sections from previously written (and probably unsuccessful) RFI documents produced for other prospective clients and pad it out by regurgitating chunks of the client's brief and accompanying documentation (i.e., stuff the client already knows). Much of the material is recycled from other documents for other clients, such as the team's résumés (CVs) and the case studies, dropped in to prove the bidding company's competency in delivering the sort of solutions this prospective client might be looking to replicate. Fatal mistake.

Recycling might be good for the planet but it is *bad* for winning new business

There is a problem with recycling content, especially content that was flawed and not very good in the first place. All clients want a bespoke answer. This means taking time, effort and trouble to think through everything you say to them from scratch. After all, if you turned up to a first date in your private life smelling of the perfume from the date you'd just finished, trotting out plainly generic questions and showing no individual care for the person in front of you, you wouldn't expect the relationship to go far, would you? So why do we do exactly this in new business?

This means that everything – E-V-E-R-Y-T-H-I-N-G – must be written from scratch. Nothing off the shelf.*

The résumés of your team need to sing the praises of the unique contribution each person will make to *this specific project or client* (preferably with a picture of that person in situ in the prospective client's store or using their service or product). The success stories (no more dull case studies) need to have specific relevance to this prospective client's business. And, as we have previously said, they need to be written as *interesting stories* rather than as bland case studies. They need to come alive with their relevance to *this specific* client, the brilliance of the work you did and the results it produced.

Here's a list of lazy, cut-and-paste practices from a company we were brought in to help. This company stuck the team résumés at the back of the RFI document and they were the same résumés they stuck in every client document regardless of that client's need or industry. In short, they were untailored. Accordingly, they were written to the standard résumé formula that so many companies use:

- A long list of important job titles and company names where this person has worked.
- A total absence of evidence that this person has personally achieved anything remarkable at said companies but a long list of hyperbolic, unsubstantiated claims about this person designed to make them sound far more dynamic and

---

* When JFK fired the starter gun on the space race by declaring that 'by the end of this decade' the USA would put a man on the moon, he galvanised the entire industrial and technological might of America behind the project. They did everything from scratch, including designing a million-dollar pen that would write at extreme temperatures, in zero gravity and never fail in the event of an emergency. The Russians used a pencil. Ho ho. Who won the space race? Everything from scratch – or you'll lose.

Einstein-like than is believable. For example: 'Sophie is a creative, hands-on (as opposed to detached and aloof?) senior marketer who has successfully (as opposed to *un*successfully?) led some of the biggest brands in retail (what, she was CEO?) and who has multi-category international experience in developing and implementing innovation, marketing and category strategy.' Blah blah blah. It doesn't *mean* anything – it's just a string of clichés squashed together.

- A jokey bit at the end to inject some personality into this otherwise one-dimensional, dry-as-dust epitaph.

The problem, apart from the fact that each résumé adheres to the same formula, is that these biographies have been used so many times and for so long that no one putting together the RFP or RFI document has read them for years – or reads them this time round. So no one spots that the supposedly 'jolly' bit at the end of each résumé now makes the team sound so tired and old-fashioned. Here's an example:

When he's not working, Steve spends his time on two wheels both on and off road or tinkering around with various old vehicles.

Tinkering around? This is such antiquated and colloquial terminology. It sounds so amateur and low energy – as if Steve will be *tinkering around* with your (the prospective client's) brand. It belongs in the 1950s rather than the twenty-first century.

Think about every word of your team's biographies. As if you were introducing them in person.

Brand your presentation

Another frequently missed opportunity to differentiate is with the title we give to our document. We know why. Time is scarce, yes? No time to be imaginative. Garbage. Don't go to all the trouble of producing the document and then fail to introduce it properly. Our American cousins are very good at this. We once pitched for Energiser batteries. The company had just launched a new titanium battery. Being rather dull Brits, we entitled our pitch 'Pitch to Energiser batteries'. Not scintillating, is it? Our Chicago-based brethren came up with: 'WELCOME TO A TITANIUM DREAM'.

Better, eh? You'd probably want to read that document and see that presentation, wouldn't you? In fact, you'd probably want to go to the cinema and watch the damn movie.

How about if this document landed in your inbox: 'Unlocking prepared vegetables and Hot Bites Category for profitable top-line growth'.

Your heart would sink, wouldn't it? You'd reach for the razor blades. It doesn't exactly sound like a page-turner. And it doesn't get any better. Here's the first paragraph from the executive summary:

A set of actionable platforms with suggested innovation, renovation and core activation initiatives, which will be compared and contrasted with existing global financial plans allowing for potential gap-closing.

A belter. That'll have them gripped. All that revoltingly over-complicated sentence actually says is: 'We're going to show you some practical new ideas which will make you grow more effectively.'

Holy cow. No wonder we don't like new business if we think it involves writing nonsense like this.

Breathing life into your words – the art of good writing

We thought it would be helpful if we showed you some examples from work we have been involved with which illustrates beautifully what we mean when we say you can deploy the English language – or any other language – very powerfully and differentiate your proposal by crafting it so it reads fluently, easily and compellingly.

The way you introduce the team is vital. Rather than just focusing on the functionality and job titles of the team, get some *attitude* into it – put some heart into your approach to putting the team together. Tell the client prospect what their business *means* to you. It doesn't have to be sycophantic, just sincere. Below is a submission we prepared for a client who was pitching for a very large assignment from a well-known brand.

The executive summary – the first thing the clients would read when they received the written submission – sets out the stall in an unconventional way. Normally, RFPs – and the verbal pitch itself – kick off with a string of platitudes:

Thank you for the opportunity to present our solutions to you. We are immensely grateful for the chance to pitch for your famous company, and if you were to work with us you would be our most important client . . . blah, blah, blah

We have worked very hard on your business over the last month and we have been unstinting in our efforts to understand both the market dynamics of your sector and to get to grips with the intricacies of your operations . . . blah, blah, blah. We feel very passionate about blah, blah, blah.

The words die on the page. It is a litany of clichés and has no soul.

Yawn.

By all means, acknowledge the scale of the opportunity but also make it *personal* to the team – invest your emotion in it. We are so scared of demonstrating emotion in the guise of being professional that we lose any connection or sincerity with the audience.

Get to the point. Use what little time you have to hit them between the eyes. Everything you write and say must create the feeling that you and your company are better and different to all the others they will see. Lift and separate your offer by using language brilliantly to set out your stall so they really want to hear what you have to say.

Like this:

For every person on this team, this has been a defining moment. Only once in our careers are we likely to get the opportunity to pitch for a brand we have all grown up with, has been part of all of our personal stories and which offers the largest canvas on which to do the finest work of our careers. For every one of us, this is personal. But we are acutely conscious that making a change in your communications partner is probably the last thing you want to do right now when you are literally and metaphorically surrounded by a world changing at white-water pace. Sometimes it's good to have a fixed point or two. So we thought it is beholden on us to make the case for why change is needed if not welcomed. These arguments are summarised below.

(There followed five well-argued reasons that changing partners was both necessary and appropriate.)

Better? You betcha it's better.

The summary concludes:

> The pressures you face at this moment are as extraordinary and testing as any previously encountered since you first arrived in the UK nearly fifty years ago. That moment of arrival represents a key inflection point in the British culinary landscape. You changed Britain forever. And there are some fascinating parallels with that era: then, we were about to join the Common Market; today we are about to leave it. Both ends of this time spectrum afford great opportunity – as well as potential threat – to the business. The revolution you started some two generations ago has, to a great extent, led the evolution of the ever-changing face of Britain.
>
> Four decades later, we are again at a genuine economic, cultural and culinary crossroads. There has never been a better or more perfect time for you to reassert your uniquely inclusive, unquestionably innovative place at the very heart of every British community. Today's presentation is all about how we accomplish that mission together.

This is a properly crafted, show-opening, rallying cry – an invitation to an exciting presentation which unifies the client's heritage and ambition for the future. Whether it makes BMWs or burgers, doorknobs or the Chrysler Building, the people who work for a company all want to be made to feel like what they do is important. They all want to feel that what they are doing is the equivalent of sending a manned mission to the moon. Your job is to make their spine straighten, their resolve stiffen, their sap rise. Using written and verbal language brilliantly, seductively, compellingly, will help them feel all of that and associate those feelings with you. Remember, it's how you make them *feel*. Raise your prose from the prosaic to the persuasive, use facts judiciously, invest your heart and soul into the mission and you will win everyone's hearts and minds – which is what the game of new business is all about.

Timidity is the enemy of new business prospecting

Giles was the newly appointed worldwide CEO for one of the world's largest communications groups. He had heard that we knew how to win new business. We were asked to write an analysis of his company's business development performance for him. We were given access to all the members of the global executive committee, to their clients and to commentators in the industry. We did a thorough and detailed job. The report we wrote was corporate, dry and anodyne and, quite rightly, they rejected it and our proposal.

Our mistake? We tried to double guess what they were prepared to hear and – a very bad mistake – write it in order to sell our solution (which was a training programme). This cynical approach backfired. The client was cross.

'Tell us what you *really* think,' he bit.

We were dispirited. They had rejected a lot of hard work which had taken ages, and we were in danger of losing the biggest contract of our company's brief life. At the time, we were facilitating a conference of mergers and acquisitions (M&A) specialists in LA. The same night we received the negative feedback to our proposal from Giles, our M&A client told us over dinner: 'What we like about you guys is you tell it how it is. It's shocking to hear but invaluable because we need to hear it and it makes us better.'

Renewed, inspired and invigorated by this vote of confidence and reminder of why we were in business, we went up to our room and spent three hours writing a brand-new document for the communications agency CEO entitled '*CRI DE COEUR*' (cry from the heart). It was direct, to the point, pithy and deeply personal. It put the cat among the pigeons. Giles lapped it up.

As a consequence, we were invited to the next meeting of the global executive board and commissioned to revolutionise the way they did their new business. By speaking our mind, by unleashing the best of ourselves, we won a much bigger job than we could have dreamed possible.

Phew. That's a lot. But it's a very big subject. Here's a quick summary just to pull out the really important points which will make your message shine:

- Each word counts and each badly chosen word costs. Choose your words – both written and spoken – carefully. Words are valuable assets, so don't squander them.
- Create a thirty-second 'elevator pitch' so you are ready at all times to give whoever asks what you do a differentiating description of who you are and how you make a difference to your clients. And make sure the whole team use the same elevator pitch. Clients like consistency.
- Be clear on your objective for each meeting. What does success look like? What do you want the client to feel, think and do as a result of meeting you?
- Don't rush to write a proposal following the meeting. Evaluate whether their request for a proposal indicates serious intent and commitment or is just a tactic to kick the can down the road.
- If you do write a proposal, make their mouth water in anticipation. Write it, don't 'rote' it.
- Tell success stories, not dry-as-dust case studies, to illustrate why you are brilliant and different.
- Tell failure stories; being honest builds trust.
- Ask for and use testimonials from existing clients. Third-party peer endorsement provides reassurance (especially to Analytical types) and creates credibility.

- Write all RFPs and RFIs from scratch. Off-the-shelf, cut-and-paste, recycled content screams laziness and lack of care and original thought. Which is death to any business seduction. In new business, recycling is bad for your future prosperity.
- Brand your presentation: 'Welcome to a Titanium Dream'; 'D-Day'; 'The Audacity of Hope'; 'Desert Storm'. Branding your idea makes it easy for the audience to remember it for long after they first see it.
- Use words to make the audience's collective spine 'go global' – your words need to stiffen them with pride at the importance of their task.

CHAPTER 13

TOOLS AND TIPS

'There are two kinds of people in the world: those who divide
everybody into two kinds of people, and those who don't'
Anonymous

Half the people reading this book will totally buy into the
'diligent farmer' approach. They will thrive on building relationships and love the idea of serendipity and being open to the
magic of chance and opportunity. The other half are thinking,
Yeah, yeah, I get that but I need a spreadsheet. I need to tick off
things every week. I love process. Help me.

Process-lovers, this chapter is for you. It includes some tools
and tips to help you make a start and keep track of your progress.

If you want to beef up your new business pipeline and you
respond well to structure, take these four steps:

1. Create your prospect list
2. Plan your approach
3. Make it happen (but make it fun)
4. Persist with it

1. CREATE YOUR PROSPECT LIST

As well as serendipitous meetings with people when you are out and about, you're likely to have a list of client companies you want to work with. At this stage, don't think about editing; this is about the creation of a longlist. Evaluating whether it's worth pursuing these companies comes later.

Here are some ideas to get you started:

Dream clients

This is where you can put Google, Nike, Tesla and Farfetch on your list (or your equivalents). These are the organisations you'd love to help. You feel an alignment between their offer, their values and yours. You know you would do an amazing job for these clients.

Commonality

Identify clients that resemble your best clients. They could be in the same sector or they could be in a different sector but have a similar need or problem that you have solved for one of your existing clients.

Common audience

Which clients have the same customers as your good clients? There will be economies of understanding and scale to be gained by reapplying your expertise across a portfolio of clients chasing similar customer profiles.

Non-pitchers

These are companies that have worked with an existing supplier for a while. Are they happy or are they stuck in a rut? It can be comparatively easy to make an existing professional services advisor look slothful when it comes to client service and proactivity if you are targeting a particular client. The chasing team is often made up of the big brains and most dynamic operators – people who are both buyable and believable. Compare this with the existing supplier's weary team, jaded through years of working with this client. A team that no longer looks forward to contact with their client (and vice versa). The client who, even now, could be seduced by your new business dream team.

Lost pitches

You lost the pitch, but it was so close – at least, that's what the client told you. Tempting as it is to shriek, 'They're dead to me!' and storm off in a huff every time the client's name is mentioned, it's worth a trip up to the higher ground and keeping in light contact with them, particularly if you got on well with them in the run up to the pitch and you lost for reasons other than chemistry. Add them to your mailing list, invite them to your events, check in with them every couple of months. You will soon know if the desire to keep in touch is mutual. If it is, you will be in prime position should the shiny new relationship with your rival who won the pitch falter. And, if nothing else, you're adding another contact to your network.

The faltering

Clients buy to avoid a loss or make a gain, so you need to understand which companies are heading for trouble. Everyone who has responsibility for business development should be devouring on a daily basis the key business and technology news, analysis and commentary. The *Financial Times*, the *Wall Street Journal, Bloomberg*, CNN's market reports, *Wired, The Economist, Fortune* magazine. You need to have an overview of the status of key business players – who's hot, who's not and why – so that you can keep an eye out for opportunity as well as being able to talk eruditely about the performance of whoever and whatever at your next meeting. If you know you can help them get out of a hole, get in contact.

The booming

Same. But for businesses who are actually doing well and might want to realign, upgrade, add to their partner relationships to match their ever-increasing requirements, fortunes and ambitions.

The weak

Which of your competitors are going through a rough patch? Who's had a revolving door of leadership and a mass exodus of clients and staff? All's fair in love and war: target their clients.

Talk to other advisors

You'll often end up working with other advisors on a client project. They could be a design team or a production agency, lawyers or accountants. Get to know what they do and help them to understand what you do. Get them to know and like you. Discuss how you could help each other out – who do they know who they could introduce you to and how could you reciprocate? In the echo chamber that is the client world, you want your clients' other professional advisors to be waxing lyrical about how brilliant you and your firm are. And if you become well connected in professional services – the realm of corporate finance, lawyers, accountants, private equity, venture capitalists, real estate and management consultancies – the voices of trusted advisors surrounding clients you want to work with can work very loudly on your behalf.

Think beyond your own market

Be flexible. If you work in corporate real estate and have historically only pursued clients who lease large office blocks, you're facing a big refocus of strategy. You can build your pipeline if you add flexible workspaces (e.g. WeWork) to the mix and move into new areas as change of use class orders come into effect and the market seeks to reabsorb the tens of millions of square feet of vacant office and retail city centre space. Where is your target market heading? What advice do they need to help reshape their physical office needs? What work patterns are going to influence real estate portfolios? Who are the new entrants coming in? Who is relatively small now but could be big – can you get in early and grow with them? Now, more than ever, we need to think laterally and imaginatively.

We once referred a lead to the UK's biggest shopper marketing agency. They declined. It was too small for them. They only worked with big fish. The little brand was called Innocent Drinks. Innocent is a pretty big player now and was bought by Coca-Cola. The shopper marketing agency? Not so big, anymore.

2. PLAN YOUR APPROACH

If you've followed these suggestions, you should have a nice long list of prospects by now. A list that can feel both overwhelming and unrealistic. Time to bring in the evaluation matrix.

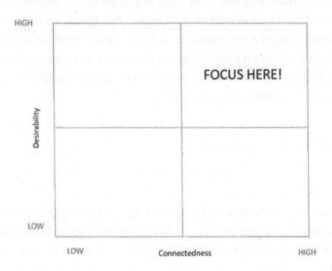

Map your prospects on the matrix using the axis of 'Desirability' (how much you want them) and 'Connectedness' (whether you have a route into that client). It could be that someone you know works there or one of your clients or team members has just got a job there, or you have mutual connections on LinkedIn. The aim is to prioritise your focus on the prospects with whom you are highly connected and who have high desirability. If the score is low on both axes, don't spend too much time on them; just stay on their radar and wait for serendipity to arrive.

Now what?

Whether you're in love with spreadsheets and know your way around a pivot cell or your Excel skills are limited to putting lines round boxes and using the sum tool, you'll need to have some sort of plan to track activity and progress.

At its most basic, you will need to keep track of your prospects and contacts: a database. How you do it is up to you. You can invest in a highly sophisticated model such as Salesforce or you can use Google Sheets. For your own sanity it should be accessible (for example, online) and intuitive.

Then, it can be helpful to set yourself some deadlines. According to a study conducted by UCL published in the *European Journal of Social Psychology*, it takes sixty-six days for a new behaviour to become automatic. In that spirit, let's start with a sixty-day plan – two months. This is less about filling in activity for every single day and more about keeping yourself accountable over a set period. As we keep reiterating, new business prospecting isn't something you can turn off and on like a switch; it should be a constant stream of day-to-day activity.

Before you start to populate your plan, think about the following:

- **Relationship mapping.** Looking back at your evaluation matrix, your prospects should be those with high desirability and connectedness. Who are they connected to? How strong are the relationships? What are you going to do to get an introduction? Who can help you? What do you need to do to improve and develop stronger relationships? Who do you need to know that you don't already (contact of a contact)?
- **Broaden understanding and value.** What are the key business issues for that prospect client? What's your own and your company's point of view? How can you help them?
- **Proactive approach.** What are you actually going to *do*? Send them something? Ask for a meeting? Go to an event

that you know they will be attending? Invite them to one of your events? Send them a personalised video explaining how you have helped a similar company and would like to discuss if you can help them in the same way? (We elaborate on this last example in Chapter 20.) Work out your contact strategy

3. MAKE IT HAPPEN (BUT MAKE IT FUN)

Louisa has kept a diary since she was fourteen. Sadly, her observations were less Samuel Pepys, more Adrian Mole (sample entry: 'Went to village shop, bought cat food.') Every entry ends with, 'Went to bed,' to eliminate any possibility of doubt, and self-awareness is low: 'Told the parents I wouldn't be moving back home after all. They took it quite well.' At the start of every year, an enthusiastic longlist of resolutions appears. Not content with one or two, throughout the 1980s she committed to a minimum of ten life-changing actions to occur before the year's end. The usual suspects regularly appear – 'lose weight, spend less' – whilst a heartfelt, 'GIVE UP GIN' was clearly written the wrong side of a hangover. By the 1990s, the list is even longer and vaguer, and is now rechristened, 'GOALS'. 'Work really hard'; 'Think about my career – like, what it's to be?'; and 'Have a good year.' (Her end of year summary comment: 'Debatable'.) One outlier appears around 1991 – 'Rave.' Reader, she did.

New business prospect lists remind us of our youthful selves: writing resolutions we wanted to achieve, but failing to do anything consistently to make them happen. Louisa still keeps a diary (she no longer captures whether she went to bed or not; it is left to the reader to assume) and she still makes resolutions. She has learned that, as with many things, less is more. Better to put down two or three significant things that you will actually put your focus and attention on to make happen, than a long list of things that you know, even as you are writing them down, you have neither the intention nor the will to make happen.

For your prospecting list to have any hope of turning into something tangible, you will need to answer these questions:

- **What are my priorities?**
- **What will stop me from achieving them? What actions do I need to take as a result?** It is better to *plan for failure* than for success. Most people write down a wish and then don't think of the obstacles to getting it fulfilled. Write down all the things that will cause you to fail and then have a strategy for overcoming each one. For example, if your priority is to go on an early morning run, the things that will cause you to fail will be: (a) ignoring your alarm; (b) the weather; (c) you can't find your running kit. So: (a) put your alarm on the other side of the bedroom last thing at night to make yourself get up and turn it off; (b) lay out a waterproof; (c) put all that you will need on the radiator next to your bed so it's ready and warm for the morning. Hey presto! Oh. And go out and run.
- **How will I track progress?** Will you measure progress in terms of the number of meetings you have each week? New contacts? Referrals? Proposals? Knowing what your goals are and keeping track of your progress helps you stay motivated. Google does it using objectives and key results (OKR). They are measured every two weeks. Google use data well and they are doing OK. Do likewise.
- **How can I make it fun?** When Louisa worked in an agency, she started each year with a list of the London restaurants she wanted to visit and made it her mission to set up new business meetings in each one. When she was leading a team of mainly single people, she positioned work events as 'how to meet your next boyfriend/girlfriend' which made them all much more likely to turn up.

Once you have the answers, you're ready to populate your sixty-day plan. You can find an example and further ideas for goal-setting in Part VI (p.275).

4. PERSIST WITH IT: YOUR SIXTY-DAY PLAN

Given that this includes weekends, the reality is that your plan will run across twelve working weeks. To keep the momentum, you should aim for at least one prospecting-related activity every day. Given that this could be as little as one email, it shouldn't prove too onerous a task. We are assuming that you have other responsibilities as well as prospecting and new business development. If that's not the case, then you probably should aim a little higher than pressing send on a solitary email before clocking off for the day.

One of the little-shared aspects of prospecting is how tedious it can be. Your emails can be ignored, people don't get back to you when they say they will, meetings get cancelled. Some days you can despair that you'll never sell anything, ever. But you will. Business development is 90 per cent persistence. Keep going, like the Duracell Bunny, when all own-label battery bunnies have conked out. To relieve the tedium of doing the same old same old, you need to mix it up a bit. When you're staring down the billowy white sheets of an empty schedule, here's a few things you can try to get an appointment:

Call or email a client you haven't talked to for two years

Remember, the aim here is not to sell them something but simply to re-establish a connection. If you got on well with them before, they are likely to be pleased to hear from you. A coffee together gives you the opportunity to catch up. Then you are back on each other's radar and it's up to you to not lose touch with them for so long again. Because next time you meet they might steer the conversation round to business and there may be a way you could be of help.

Send a handwritten card

Wow. Radical. In this digital age, the only post we get nowadays consists of catalogues and bills. As a result, anything hand-written landing on the desk will always stand out and is mildly exciting, too. Send a card to the person you want to meet and something relevant (books are good but if the budget doesn't allow, an interesting and pertinent press clipping or magazine can also work). Years ago, the Royal Mail had a very successful advertising campaign with the strapline, 'Saw this and thought of you.' Who doesn't feel special when someone has thought of them? Dig out your fountain pen and get cracking.

Send a thank you gift to someone who referred you

They're much more likely to do it again if you express gratitude. Plus, it's good manners.

Email the editor of a newspaper or magazine your clients read

The most on-target magazine for our company to feature in has been British Airways' *Business Life*. For eighteen months, we had an editorial page within the magazine, and every time our thoughts were published, we got a number of emails and enquiries as a result. It turns out that not only are BA's business travellers a literally captive audience for the magazine, but they are also a curious and interested bunch of people – just like you, and just like the type of clients you want to attract. Next time you are on board, pick up a copy, read it and respond with your point of view by sending an email to the editor. There's even the incentive of winning 'letter of the month' (with often a decent prize attached) to encourage you further. And if you agree, disagree or want to know more from the author of an article, contact them – most people are delighted to get feedback from readers and appreciate you making the effort. What's the most on-target publication to reach your potential clients?

Add fifteen people to your database

Go back through your emails and diary for the last month and check that everyone you contacted is in your database. Take a ridiculous amount of satisfaction in watching those database numbers increase every month – YOU ARE BUILDING YOUR NETWORK!

LinkedIn

There are many tools available to the networker and new-business builder. LinkedIn is one of the best. It basically keeps your database for you, and with an investment of just fifteen minutes a day spent on the platform, you will be kept in the daily flow of business information running through your personal community and the communities of your personal network's network.

When you appear on someone's radar, your LinkedIn profile is almost certainly their first port of call for research. It is also your primary tool for research when you are investigating people who you want to connect with or are lined up to meet. You can learn enormous amounts about people just by reading their LinkedIn profile – not only the jobs they have had, interests they espouse, which groups they follow, articles and comments they have made; but also, if your own radar is on, from how it looks, how it reads and by the style of the comments they make on other people's content. To the keen-eyed prospector, LinkedIn is a diamond mine.

In terms of building your network, your best bet is to look at your existing contacts and see who knows whom – if there are particular people that you think would be interesting to know and who might benefit from your product or service, you can ask your contact to make an introduction. We refer to several good and bad examples of people's profiles on LinkedIn in Chapter 18. As a rule, it's worth spending a few hours to get your personal profile looking and sounding good. Writing articles on Linkedin or republishing your blog posts there (or just sharing an article written by someone which you like and adding your own comment on the issue) are quick ways to become active and show interesting stuff to the deliberate browser (and there are lots of them). The main thing, though, is to get into the habit of visiting it every day and to take part.

If you've got this far, you really are a process fan. Of the behavioural styles we featured earlier, it's likely you favour the Analytical style; you are no stranger to a spreadsheet and are fond of logic and order. So, we'll end this chapter with an approach we believe you will appreciate: the summary. (And for all the Drivers who skipped to the end of this chapter, 'Hello.')

Your four-step guide to successful prospecting:

1. Create your prospect list
Use the wisdom of the crowd. If there are others in your company besides you, get them involved as you create your longlist. You never know who knows who. There's many a company that has been grateful for the introduction one of their account executives gave them to their godmother who just happened to be marketing director for a global packaged goods business.

2. Plan your approach

Be realistic. Edit. By all means, have a couple of 'moonshot' clients in there, but focus the majority of your attention on the clients that are both desirable and with whom you either have some existing relationship or a 'six degrees of separation' approach to making contact.

3. Make it happen (but make it fun)

Set some goals and agree how you will track them. Incentivise yourself and others to make it as fun as you can. Meetings don't always need to be in the office. Make it stimulating for yourself and the prospect – can you meet at a new restaurant, a cool coffee shop or go for a walk in a different environment? Promise and deliver speed. If you say you will only meet for twenty minutes, do it. Your prospect will be eternally grateful.

4. Persist with it

@rmccarthyjames wrote on Twitter, 'All of my plans for the future involve me waking up tomorrow with a sudden sense of discipline and adherence to routine that I have never displayed even once in my life'.

If this is you too, you are going to have to start small. Set yourself realistic goals – the one or two things you will do every day and build it up from there. If you're in a new business role in a big corporate organisation and you're a bit @rmccarthyjames, you're probably not in a job that plays to your strengths. And if you're working for yourself, you'll probably find that, like Victor Hugo, 'Nothing makes a man so adventurous as an empty pocket' and, it turns out, you do have a sudden sense of discipline and adherence to routine after all.

CHAPTER 14

HOW TO GET MORE LEADS

'I feel that luck is preparation meeting opportunity'
Oprah Winfrey

In addition to networking – or, as we call it, talking to strangers
– these are the most effective ways of getting new leads:

- Recommendations from existing clients
- Reputation and word of mouth
- Clients moving to new jobs
- Personal contacts
- Media coverage
- Intermediaries
- Online targeting (see Chapter 20)

Let's take these one by one and look at practical ways to accelerate the number of relevant leads that can come your way from
each.

Recommendations from existing clients

Imagine the scenario. You're at the end of a client project. You
and the team have done a fantastic job. Late nights, long hours,
even some weekend work, but it's all worth it as the project has

been delivered and you are now basking in the glow of a job well done. Sit back and wait for your client to recommend you to everyone they know. And wait. And wait.

It's not that the client doesn't want to help; sometimes they do. But we're all busy people and the minute one project is over, another comes up. Making time to make a recommendation can quickly slip down the agenda, to be filed under 'never going to happen'.

So what can you do to help? The first thing you can do to improve the number of recommendations you get from existing clients is to ask them to recommend you. It is as simple as that. Most of the time we don't ask our clients for help due to a number of reasons. We may feel that doing good work is enough to get us noticed and therefore recommended. And yes, sometimes it is, but that's a very passive approach to take. We may feel at worst embarrassed and at best a bit sheepish to ask. Doesn't it feel a bit grasping? Well, no. Not if you couch it in the right terms.

All you need to say is, 'Who else can we help?' Or, in more detail, 'We've done a great job for you, this is work that we enjoy doing and are good at. Is there anyone else in your network that has a similar issue that you would recommend us to?'

What you're looking for is your client to open their contacts book and either:

- Make the introduction themselves, via email, connecting both parties, so you can continue the conversation without them;
- Provide *you* with the contact details so that you can contact your client's contact directly, but copy the client in so it is a 'warm' lead – one that has not come out of the blue but one that has been passed on knowingly.

By the way:

**91 per cent of customers say they'd give referrals.
Only 11 per cent of salespeople ask for referrals***

Easy win. Ask. Don't make your old clients work hard to keep in touch with you. You keep in touch with them – and ask them for referrals. It will keep your pipeline topped up with new names. But remember to ask when your client still loves you!

If you do get recommended and it leads to paid work, say thank you. Louisa was once asked by a friend's sister, who was a CEO, to recommend a PR agency who could run their annual awards ceremony. She thought of an ex-colleague who had recently moved to a new agency outside London. Louisa made the introduction and heard nothing more so assumed nothing had come of it. Fast-forward eighteen months and she met up with the ex-colleague who had got in touch as she was up in London. Turns out she was in London to have a meeting about the awards ceremony because the agency had been working on it for the past year. Louisa had no idea. As a result of her recommendation, her ex-colleague brought in a new six-figure client without a pitch. A thank you would have been nice. Will Louisa recommend her again? Call her petty, but no.

Reputation and word of mouth

Whether you are a sole trader or work within a multinational, your business success lives and dies on your reputation. As Warren Buffett said, 'It takes twenty years to build a reputation and five minutes to ruin it. If you think about that, you'll do things differently.'

* Dale Carnegie, *How to Win Friends and Influence People* (New York: Simon & Schuster, 1936).

Ultimately, you want people to talk about you positively and in a way that is helpful to you. So it is worth investing the time and thought into what that might be and then ensure that every interaction you have delivers on that promise.

Our purpose in writing this book is to stimulate business for the greatest number of people so it does the greatest amount of good. Our target audience is those people who are impatient to grow. Our tone of voice is to be 'respectfully disrespectful' – and to stimulate the reader with practicable new ideas to help them network and generate new business. We behave with heart and conscience; we don't ever recommend people do things we don't believe in or haven't done ourselves. We hope we are known in the marketplace for being all of these things. Oh. And for being quick.

What are you known for?

Clients moving to new jobs

A client moving to a new job is a bit like one of those wooden weather house barometers. On one side of the house is a woman; on the other a man. One comes out when the sun shines and one comes out when it rains. But they never come out at the same time. Similarly, your favourite client moves to a new job and takes you with them but the new client coming in, to replace them, sacks your company to bring in their favourite advisors. Or, worst-case scenario, the new client sacks your company and your existing client moves to a new job where your services are not required or are being catered for by a competitor. In which case the wooden weather house barometer analogy completely breaks down. All you know is, the outlook is gloomy.

But let's not be too negative, let's look at this as an opportunity. Here's another place where you may have to play a long game.

Assuming you have a good relationship with this client, you will have no doubt given them a good send-off. Depending on the time you or your company has worked with them, the strength of the relationship, and – let's face it – the value of the business, this send-off could range from a flash party to a bunch of flowers and a heartfelt card or just an email wishing them well. The point is you want to leave each other on good terms and you want to keep in touch.

The amount of energy and enthusiasm you will have for keeping in touch will depend, frankly, on how much you like them and how well you get on with them. It's human nature to want to spend time with people we have good rapport with. These are the people that you arrange to meet for coffee or Zoom every few months. These are the people that you take out for lunch. And these are the people that you meet with no other agenda but to find out how they are and what they are up to. (Don't be the person that only gets in touch when they want something – remember what happened to Adam.) If you have maintained regular contact and communication (this could be every few weeks or, more likely, months; any longer than a year between contact can get awkward), then you will be 'top of mind and tip of tongue' when the time comes that your (ex) client needs help. And that is what you are aiming to achieve.

What about everyone else? What about the clients that have moved on to new roles with whom you have a good professional relationship, but you're never going to be lifelong friends? The same principles apply, only without the coffees and the lunches. You need to keep in regular contact. This is where you bring in your marketing team if you have one, or you create 'social excuses' – reasons to get in touch again. It could be a comment on their recent speech in an online forum, dropping the name of a mutual contact or asking if you can interview them for your new book (on a subject of interest to them). The point is: be inventive and think from their point of view about what they would find valuable or helpful or interesting. But keep in regular contact.

Keep track of your clients, your ex-clients, your fellow travellers, your associates and your well-connected friends on an Excel spreadsheet. Yes, I know, how bleeding obvious is that? But it doesn't always happen. Over the years, we have tried many and various apps, contact management systems, Trello boards, and old-fashioned address books, and if you want to save time and your own sanity, just put your contacts on a spreadsheet and ensure you update it as soon as you know someone's moved on. That is all. Don't make it your master, the purpose of your job or the *raison d'être* of your business development strategy. It is a useful tool to help you keep in touch and remind you of what you said and did last time you were in touch. It is not metadata, the Big Brother of information, or a job creation scheme for closet bureaucrats.

Once you have your spreadsheet, you can cut it any way you see fit to create new tabs and categories so that the right people get the right communications from you. Whether you're inviting your top fifty clients to a breakfast briefing or ensuring everyone you've ever met gets the link to that article you've just had published in the *Financial Times*, your spreadsheet is your friend. It is not your master.

Personal contacts

'A friend in need . . . is a pest' –
traditional Yorkshire wisdom

Is it really prospecting if it's someone you know? Well, it never hurts for your friends to know a bit about what you do – you never know, they might need what you do one day. Our first big client came via a friend who had a conference to organise, and our first book had a quote on the cover from another friend which was read by a friend of his who just happened to be the head of fixed income at the bank BNP Paribas. They became our longest-standing client. We would argue that, yes, it still counts as prospecting. Like we say, you never know where the next opportunity might come from, including from friends.

Is it better or worse if they are in your family? Only you can decide. Most people steer clear of tapping up their family for business, for good reasons. But there may be people in your friendship group or family who know someone that you don't who could benefit from your company's service. If that's the case, a polite request for an introduction is worth making. But if your request gets politely ignored or rebuffed, then don't push it. Accept that your family member is saying without words that they don't want to do this. Move on to strangers instead. Which leads us to . . .

Media coverage

Any positive media coverage is a third-party endorsement. You are effectively saying, 'Don't just take my word for it; here's what someone (trusted, credible, reliable) says about us.' This is the ecosystem that you need to create, both digitally and in the analogue world.

Whether you want to admit it or not, you are already engaging in public relations activity. People and companies communicate through the customer (client) experience, how you treat your employees, activities and events you may run for industry groups, your social media feeds and any marketing activity (emails, newsletters, brochures, etc.). Your most powerful communication resides in the good things people say about you in media that other people trust. By deciding to take a more proactive approach to PR, you take ownership of activity that is already happening but are being more strategic and intentional about it.

One of the issues that PR agency clients struggle to understand is the fact that the media works to its own agenda. Just because you think that your business is worthy of an article in the *Financial Times*, doesn't mean it's going to happen. You need a 'hook' – a reason your story is relevant. If it all feels too much like hard work to know where to start, consider using a freelance PR expert to help you. Many freelancers have worked in big agencies on high-profile accounts and bring that experience to a role where they can be much more flexible and hands-on than they were in their previous corporate role. You can benefit from their expertise ahead of signing up to a long and potentially expensive contract with an agency.

However, if you do want to DIY your PR efforts – and it is best if you do because journalists want a relationship with you, not a mouthpiece – make it manageable and achievable. Focus on a small media list of titles and broadcast channels that you know your clients engage with, and approach them. For broadcast, put yourself forward as someone willing to comment on a particular set of subjects. Be a go-to expert on a narrow set of subjects. Find the appropriate news channels or magazine shows and forward a very brief biography with a photo and your contact details. When they ring you for the first time, make sure you drop everything to make the interview. If it goes well, you'll be in the virtual address book for next time. Like many of us, journalists love a shortcut. If they can find an expert on sustainable energy or town planning or automotive or retail who is willing to make themselves available at short notice, why wouldn't they keep using that person rather than doing numerous ring rounds and emails to find someone new? That's why, if you take notice of these things, you see the same old 'talking heads' being wheeled out time and again. Why shouldn't one of those be you?

For digital or print media, remember that what goes for clients also goes for journalists. Get to them when they need you. Journalists need you – but mainly your ideas – first thing in the morning just before they go into the daily planning meeting with the editor. Pitch them your idea at 8.30 a.m. and they are prepped to pitch it to the editor thirty minutes later. By 10 a.m. you've got your commission or your story.

When you do get media coverage, what will you do with it? It's rare for a small business or sole trader to get significant media coverage without it being a high-profile story. As this quote, attributed to George Orwell, says: 'Journalism is printing what somebody else does not want printed; everything else is public relations.' Often, the coverage you'll get is limited to a quote, a couple of lines of your thoughts plus your name and, if you are lucky, your company name and a description of what you do. We hate to break it to you, but this is unlikely to get the phones ringing off the hook with potential clients desperate for your services.

But you can use this coverage on your social media platforms, within emails to clients and to prospects. It carries more weight than you alone saying how great you are: here is a trusted media source valuing your commentary. It positions you as an expert and underlines your credibility. This is all very helpful and it provides another 'excuse' to get in contact with prospects.

The other use of media is access to privileged information ahead of publication, if your media contacts are in the know. Early access to news can give you excuses to get in touch with the prospect because there is something they might need help to sort out or exploit – something they may or may not have spotted.

Intermediaries

Many sectors that rely on hiring and working with professional service providers look to intermediaries to help them choose a potential partner. Intermediaries act as a matchmaker between client and advisor. They often have no formal role in the decision-making, but act as umpire to ensure the process is fair for both parties. They might be influential and their word will count. Sometimes, you pay a fee to the intermediary and they will put you on the shortlist if they feel you are right for a particular brief. Other times, the commissioning client pays for the intermediary. Either way, you will have to invest time building the relationship with your contact at the intermediary too. It's not enough to send over your credentials and assume you will be top of mind from that day forward. If you think this could be useful to you, contact a couple of intermediaries, speak to others who use them and decide if it's worth the investment. For the bigger pitches, intermediaries can be a way of being catapulted onto a shortlist – without them you wouldn't even be on the prospect client's radar. In certain industries, intermediaries can be very important. They are the guardians to clients and they guard this access jealousy. Try and woo them, make them your friends, seek out their counsel. They are often quite incisive about how you are seen by clients and they appreciate being asked for their opinion. Like most people.

WHEN EVERYONE ZIGS, YOU MUST ZAG

We believe that you can be efficient at doing what everyone else is doing or you can change the rules, do it a different way and, in so doing, be much more effective. Surely it is cleverer to innovate if everyone else is sticking to the conventions? Do things that make you stand apart, be memorable, create a relationship so the other person might want to pursue you rather than you pursuing them.

Below are some ways to innovate, to get more leads and accelerate your contacts from stone cold to warm. After all, you can only start to cook when things begin to heat up.

1. Don't go to your own industry trade show, go to theirs

Until the advent of COVID-19, there were loads of conferences and trade events taking place around the world every week. As the business world has had to adjust, many events have been postponed, cancelled or moved online. New strictures on travel and large public gatherings allied to the adoption of new practices as normal – such as moving to online meetings rather than in-person – have changed this landscape, probably for ever. Many industries have taken the opportunity to reinvent such events online. The fashion industry, for example, has done this very effectively, decamping from expensive and environmentally unsustainable roadshows in Milan, New York, London and Paris to virtual shows hosted online, without suffering any discernible commercial damage. Indeed, this new model, forced on them by the pandemic, is now being hailed as the new way of doing business in that industry.

Motor shows have also been forced to reconfigure. The big manufacturers are pulling out of what were, for decades, must-attend events. This is not just thanks to COVID-19 restrictions, but also to endemic declines in audience numbers and the decreasing relevance of static car shows in a world of new mobility challenges, improved virtual experiences and universal accessibility to product information and demonstrations online.

In such a changing world, it is the job of new business generators to make the new formats work for us. In a world where content is king, online conference organisers will be even more keen to show what value they can add as a reason for people to attend their virtual shows and exhibitions. It will be a target-rich opportunity for those willing to offer interesting perspectives on a virtual podium via keynote speeches, online panels, vlogs and discussion groups. And it is far easier to participate in online events, to have a say via Q&A discussions and live Twitter feeds. During the period when pretty much all business was conducted online, at our consultancy we spoke in many online forums and conferences about myriad subjects: customer service, marketing myths, how to network online and branding issues. Additionally, we hosted think-ins for issues of interest and relevance to different organisations and industry leaders (such as improving the written output of the company) and we have run discussion rooms to help different organisations discuss the changes facing them in the decade ahead.

Out of all crises come opportunities.

That said, there will still be a need for industries to gather aside from the purpose of sharing information – which can be achieved online just as effectively – but to meet, break bread with one another, gossip, do deals in back rooms, catch up socially, headhunt, create new opportunities, make connections and generally share the common purpose of their chosen profession. Those who say that face to face is dead are wrong.

However, the pandemic has certainly forced a reappraisal of how we do business: is the office an unnecessary (or, at least, a reducible and renegotiable) expense? Is open plan a thing of the past? These are all opportunities for real estate firms as well as threats. We won't hop on a plane quite so readily as we did. Yes, the way we do business will alter. There are alternative and more cost-effective ways to do business which will make a huge impact on the economic landscape and on how we interact. These will continue and grow. But people still like doing business with other people, face to face. They like being together. They like the handshake, the eye contact. The ability to read body language and not just the document or the face on a screen is still an essential part of human interaction. It is still an essential part of doing business together with others. From now on, we will be doing business, networking and prospecting both online and in the physical world – and the methodology we espouse will still apply in both worlds.

The big events, the important ones where people feel they get value from meeting together, will still have relevance and still be wonderful places to network and prospect. There are contacts and opportunities to be had if you go out and visit the places where your prospect clients congregate. There will be interesting perspectives about their industry that you will learn and be able to use as an excuse to get in touch directly afterwards. Even if these events are online, it is still worthwhile attending to become more acquainted with what these people are talking and worrying about. Making the time to expand your knowledge is just as valid a reason for spending time at your prospects' trade shows and conferences as actually getting to meet them. Mainly because your competitors probably won't be there, which will give you the chance to catalyse like crazy.

If you work in real estate, the big show is Le Marché International des Professionnels de L'immobilier (MIPIM). If you're in consumer technology, it's CES in Las Vegas. These events are the ones attended by the top executives of the organisations you want to do business with. If you attend these events as a professional services advisor, chances are (a) none of your competitors are there so you have the clients to yourselves; and (b) if you walk the halls day after day and do your research to ascertain when top people might be on their exhibition stands, you might, if you have enough chutzpah, get to meet them. Even if you don't, you will hear their speeches and announcements, attend their press conferences and see their new product launches. This will give you the opportunity to form an opinion, which perhaps you could express to them or post in a blog or podcast, all of which can be used as ammunition to drive relevant dialogue afterwards. The benefit of attending is to make personal contact. Often, that requires you to push yourself forward to create that 'happy coincidence' of bumping into the person you want to meet. As the man said, 80 per cent of life is showing up. But it takes planning and nerve.

Here's an example of why.

We were once chasing to win a client in the apparel industry. Ideally, we wanted a jeans manufacturer because we had haute couture and clothes retail clients, but we had a gap in budget fashion and we wanted to fill that gap. We approached all the usual suspects. Needless to say, given they were all being chased by all our competitors, we were met with a wall of indifference to our overtures. So we went down the road to the Fashion Trade Show in Olympia to see who we could bump into. We tramped from exhibition stand to exhibition stand. Eventually, we happened upon the stand for a brand which we had been chasing for months. The person we had been trying to speak with was there. We introduced ourselves and he instantly recognised where we were from.

'You are very persistent,' he said, smiling. 'To be honest, it's very impressive you are here. No one comes to this show, not even our existing supplier!' he continued. We chatted on and then bowed out as he was clearly in demand on his company's stand, being the most senior person there. We had gone from an anonymous suitor to having a face, a presence and an identity in his mind. We left, promising that we would love to help if there was ever anything he felt an independent perspective on would be valuable.

Two weeks later, he put the business up for pitch – he was clearly dissatisfied with his current supplier, a feeling we could understand as the work they were producing for his brand was self-indulgent, vapid nonsense. Seeing it play on screen in the cinema (it was an advertising campaign) and experiencing people actually laughing at how bad it was in the audience, is what made us think they might be a good company to talk to in the first place.

We were invited onto the pitch list. Which we lost.

But we stayed in touch and when the next pitch came around, we were invited again and won. As the other man said, keep showing up.

2. When the going gets tough, the tough go for an orange juice

Richmond Events run forums for client companies to meet potential professional service advisors. They used to charter a big cruise liner to take all the delegates offshore. The environment on board was intense – advisory companies could meet potential clients face to face and no one could get away!

As an advisory company, you paid your fare and in return you were given half-hour, face-to-face meetings with people representing client organisations you wanted to impress. Additionally, you hosted a table every breakfast, lunch and dinner for the duration of the three-day voyage, and different people would be seated with you for every meal. That way it was possible to make official contact with about ten companies per day in the half-hour meetings and another eighteen people a day at mealtimes on your table. It was exhausting. It was also very expensive – client delegates went for free, enticed by on-board seminars from eminent speakers and being able to preselect those companies they were interested in meeting. The organisers ran a large 'dating' programme to try to match up suppliers with clients they wanted to meet and vice versa.

Before you boarded you were sent a list of all the people you had meetings with and a list of all the people who would be on your table for one of the mealtimes. You did your homework and tried to work out how to conduct each meeting. The list was always sent out in time to allow you to contact the people you were meeting in advance to ask them if they had a specific issue they wanted to discuss so you could prepare beforehand.

Once you were on board, the serial networking began. As soon as the ship's bell rang to signal the start of the first meeting, a forest of laptop lids went up. PowerPoint presentation after PowerPoint presentation was given to glassy-eyed clients.

There had to be a better way.

Before boarding, we had made the decision not to take a laptop into the meetings. We wanted to stand out. So we made a conscious decision to position ourselves as the place you wanted to go to if you wanted a rest from all this incessant and unimaginative selling. We became helpful to the people visiting us. We always began by saying, 'You must be fed up with PowerPoint presentations and screens – shall we grab an orange juice, go for a walk outside on the deck and just have a chat about things?'

They always leapt at the opportunity and appreciated the chance to stretch their legs. Plus, because we had done our homework on each and every client person we were scheduled to see, we could sound knowledgeable and have an intelligent perspective on the issues they might be grappling with at the time. Our intent was to cue up a follow-up conversation once we were back on land, and to try to extract one or two issues they were struggling with where a fresh viewpoint might be helpful.

Over dinner, where our guests were people we had *really* wanted to meet but who had gone for half-hour slots with other companies (the half-hour slots, weirdly, were seen as the premium meetings), we just wanted to ensure they had fun and enjoyed a respite from the relentless attentions of people wanting something from them. We figured that if we left them laughing, having enjoyed their meal more than any other meal they had on board, it would help us by making them feel well disposed to us. As the catalysts at the dining table, we always sought to create the right chemistry between us and our guests and between our guests and the other guests at our table. Chemistry is created by being likeable and intelligent conversationalists, thoughtful and attentive hosts, as well as by having something the clients might need. We were good at generating intelligent conversation around the table, and once we were back on land we had no problem fixing follow-up meetings with both our table guests and those we had treated to an orange juice.

Make the environment work for you by making it work for your prospective client. Help them to enjoy it and if they do, they will associate that enjoyment with you. Remember: it's how you make them *feel*.

3. Walk in my shoes

Email is a joy and a curse. If you do it right, it can be used to prospect and drive dialogue with a prospective client, but there are other ways to get noticed. On the same principle of zigging whilst others zag, the point of contacting someone is first to be noticed and logged as relevant; and second, to be interesting enough to create a meeting or an opportunity for a meeting. Human beings tend to notice and react to the novel and the unusual.

A few of the companies we have come across have approached the issue of how to strike up a conversation from a lateral perspective. One of the companies we worked with had Nike as a client. The work they did for Nike was very visible, well regarded and they had written it up as an interesting story which had myriad lessons for challenger brands on how to hijack an environment and gain a disproportionate level of attention and admiration relative to spend. They could have simply emailed invitations to prospective clients at other organisations to see the case study – to tell them it as a story. But these are busy people and an email is easy to delete. Instead, they used to call up the PA of the most senior person they wanted to talk with and, after a bit of a preamble, ask if that person would mind finding out what shoe size their boss had. It was such an unusual request that mostly they got the information. A few days later, a Nike box would arrive on their desk and inside would be a brand-new, latest technology, Nike trainer – but only one. With a note:

> Hi Pardeep. Wouldn't you like to be in Nike's shoes right now? With this Air Vapormax Plus you are halfway there. To get the other shoe, we'd like to invite you into our offices to hear how we can make $10 work like $20. Call us on 1234567890. The worst that can happen is you get a brand-new pair of the best trainers in the world.

It didn't always result in a meeting. But even when it didn't, it raised a laugh and usually got us into dialogue. It created the chance for a catalytic conversation.

Another organisation we know sent a new pair of walking shoes with a map showing how to walk from the recipient's offices to their own across town with the admonishment that 'A walk usually does you good. A walk to us will definitely do you good. Here's a map of how to find us, we'd love to talk with you about Brand X. It won't even cost you any shoe leather.'

Was it cheeky? Yes. Tongue in cheek? Yes. Did it help us stand out from the usual crowd? Definitely. This company was the star new business performer in a global network of over 150 offices including Paris, New York, Shanghai, Berlin and London. This office was in Birmingham, UK, and people came from all over the network to see how they did new business. This is how they did it: they stood out, did their own thing, made friends and influenced people by sticking their neck out, not trying to be too cool and daring to take a risk.

4. Don't let anyone stop you

There was an old colleague of ours who was known as 'The Preacher' because he always wore black. From head to foot. His company worked for General Electric (GE) and did the direct marketing for one of their divisions. The Preacher's direct marketing delivered outstanding results for his client and one day, after a particularly good meeting, he asked his client if there were any other division heads who he felt might benefit from the sort of work The Preacher had been doing for his client. The client thought for a minute and then came up with a name of his colleague in one of the other divisions.

'Would you let me use your name to introduce myself please?' asked The Preacher. He was given permission. He immediately tried to contact the person via phone, email, you name it. Nothing.

The Preacher made it his business to know the conferences and events that the person he wanted to talk with attended. One of them was the CES in Las Vegas, held in January. The Preacher managed to find out which flight this guy was travelling to the event on and booked himself a ticket on the same flight. Knowing the man by sight, he waited until the flight was airborne to walk down the aisle, introduce himself and mention that he had saved his client – a colleague at GE known to him – $150,000 in his direct marketing costs and felt he might be able to do the same, if not better, for this guy. He asked for two minutes to explain how and if the man didn't want to hear anything else then The Preacher would return to his seat and never bother him again. The man from GE heard enough in those two minutes to pique his interest. A follow-up meeting was scheduled and business was done.

Chutzpah.

Passion persuades and the passion to help *if you truly believe you can help*, propels you to try harder and go further than the other guy. Persistence and passion are deadly in new business. They sweep all before them. But you have to have the nerve and the courage of your convictions to see it through. Most people do not. For the few who have the appetite, the zeal and the nerve to try, try and try again, the rewards are plentiful.

These stories are remarkable. They are remarkable because most people simply do not have the courage to do new business like this – to do it differently and to keep on going. It's just too hard. It's just too embarrassing. It's just 'not the kind of person I am'. But remarkable people behaving in a remarkable way deliver remarkable results. Ordinary people doing ordinary things just deliver – surprise, surprise – ordinary results. And no one gets rewarded for ordinary results.

The chase is supposed to be thrilling. That means it will feel uncomfortable sometimes, it will feel a little hazardous and a little dangerous because it could go either way. It should feel like a roller-coaster ride. Get used to it. Soon it becomes a way of being and once you can do it for fun, well, you are playing at the top level.

CHAPTER 15

SUMMARY AND WHAT TO EXPECT FROM PART IV

Any new business effort must be actively supported, endorsed and prioritised by the CEO, otherwise it won't work

There is, unfortunately, no way around this. If you don't have the visible and loud endorsement of your efforts by the CEO you will be wasting a lot of your time on office politics, ego management and turf wars. Given that new business is the lifeblood of any company, it really should have the CEO's attention. If it doesn't, that's another red flag.

Plan for failure. Identify what's getting in the way and come up with a plan of how to overcome each and every barrier

Face reality before you start. In Part VI you'll find a chart which itemises the common barriers to success and allows you to rank them by importance for your organisation. You may have some that are unique to your organisation – add them in. Gather your senior team together and rate yourself – one is poor and five is world class – to determine where you think you are. The important part is to agree among yourselves what you are going to do to overcome each barrier.

Ensure your shop window is dazzling. Every detail matters

If you have an office, visit it as if you are a prospect. Imagine what they are thinking when they come in through the front door. What do they see? How are they greeted? Is the carpet on the stairs tatty? Are people friendly and say hello or do they avoid eye contact? Is there a buzz of activity or does it have all the atmosphere of a morgue?

Do the same for your digital office – your website, your social media channels. What do you see? What is the company saying? Is it clear or are you tangled up in jargon? Ensure any company communication is succinct, interesting, attractive and crystal clear.

And, in the same spirit, do things personally that make you stand apart from your competition; be memorable and create a relationship so the other person might want to pursue you, rather than you pursuing them.

Hone your elevator pitch

What do you actually do to help businesses? Why are you different and better than your competition? And if you aren't particularly different from your competition, what makes you distinctive? For instance, Volvo is no safer than any other major motor manufacturers but if you were to ask a group of middle-age car drivers what the attribute they most associate with Volvo, it's likely to be safety. Because for years Volvo focused on communicating that to car drivers. Successful brands focus consistently on an image and an experience they want to be recognised and valued for by clients, stakeholders and employees. Apple doesn't 'own' creativity, cool design and user-friendly products; Samsung can lay claim to those too. But Apple has created a distinctive brand around these attributes by the focus they have put on them (the stores, the friendly assistants, the 'wow' factor at launches, etc.). All these elements form a distinctive impression of the Apple brand which most of us would struggle to articulate clearly but which we all know and recognise.

Be front-footed

Just because you've done great work for a client it doesn't mean they will recommend you to others. They may not even think of it. Get in the habit of asking for referrals, recommendations and testimonials.

Side note: on days when motivation is low, read those testimonials. As Louisa's sister says, 'If ever I'm feeling down, I read my eBay feedback and feel much better.'

Then get your shop window to work for you – do your own PR to build reputation and word of mouth. One of the consistent themes in this book is there is no room for passivity in new business. Be proactive or else you'll perish. If you really believe you can help, be like The Preacher. Try harder and go further than 'the other guy' – fortune favours the one who tries harder and has more guts.

Don't cut and paste

Recycling may be good for the planet but it is bad for business. For RFPs in particular, don't cut and paste; think from the client's point of view and start afresh. Make it interesting, compelling and very well written so your RFP connects personally with the reader.

Track your progress

Be consistent with your activity and track your progress. Keep it all in one place and up to date – it need not be more complicated than that. On the days when it seems it's one rejection after another, it can be motivating to look back at your progress so keep a total of value of the new business you've brought in. Also, very useful when negotiating your annual pay rise.

WHAT TO EXPECT FROM PART IV

This is where we bring it all together and put theory into practice. You're meeting your prospect for the first time – how do you make the most of that opportunity? We'll show you how to ace it.

We'll cover some techniques to help you find out exactly what your prospect needs (even if that is something they hadn't originally thought of) so that you can expand the scope of how you could help.

We'll show how sometimes breaking the 'rules' (often self-assumed restrictions that don't even exist) can help accelerate decision-making.

And, in a world which is increasingly being lived online, we'll demonstrate how it's possible to make valuable connections without even meeting IRL.

Finally, because there is no such thing as a 100 per cent new business success rate, we'll tell you when to throw in the towel, save your energy and move on to something else. We preach 'never give up' but sometimes it is helpful to press pause.

PART IV

CONVERSION: TURN CONTACTS INTO CONTRACTS

CHAPTER 16

FIND OUT WHAT THE·Y *REALLY* NEED, SO YOU CAN HELP

'Help me help you'
Jerry Maguire, *Jerry Maguire*

Being helpful is the aim. If you think you can help, and are willing to do so, then you are not being cynical. But knowing how to steer a conversation is a useful skill because it helps the person you are talking with realise that you can help them and so move towards a potential solution to their issue. People who are great at helping do these three things:

1. They help their prospect identify their prospect's *real* needs
2. They *expand* their prospect's real needs
3. They create *new* needs

It's all about needs. Let's look at these in turn.

1. Help identify the prospect's *real* needs

The prospect may come to you with their stated needs. This is what they believe they need from you. They have a brief and they think you can answer it.

At this stage in the process your job is to listen to the brief and check with them that you have understood it correctly. If you have, then you have established that both parties are clear on the stated needs. You could stop here and offer your solution. If you take everything at face value – they want X and you can supply it – you can make the sale. If you do, it's likely to be a low-value sale and you'll be seen as a service provider rather than a trusted advisor adding value at a higher cost.

If you want to create a higher-value sale you don't stop there. Like a good doctor seeking to make a diagnosis, you will ask questions to explore the situation further. Rush ahead and you will misdiagnose. And that usually ends in a mess. By asking probing questions, you will uncover hidden needs – their real needs. These are needs the prospect didn't know they had. You've spotted it because you have experience and knowledge that the client doesn't have. Identify those needs and make them known to the client. This is what the funeral director did with David Meister in our story earlier; by probing with questions about David's accent and his aunt's status in the USA, the funeral director uncovered David's hidden real needs, which were not just to take care of his aunt's body and funeral arrangements, but to do so in accordance with the law.

Now both parties are clear on what the *real* needs are, rather than what was originally stated or written in the brief. For the prospect, this can be a light-bulb moment – you've helped them identify something they didn't know they needed until now, or brought in new information that changes their perception of what they now need.

As the examples in professional services will differ depending on sector, we're going to give the real-life example of how Louisa was expertly upsold by this method and was happy to pay a 20 per cent premium for the privilege. Let's hear it from her:

I have a tiny garden built on a slope. I wanted it levelled out so that I could put a table tennis table out there for my teenage boys to use. That was the brief. In classic purchasing style, I asked for quotes from three suppliers. They all came round to look at the garden and talk to me. The first two said, 'If you want the garden levelled off, I can do it – it will cost £X and take ten days.' But the third guy asked me, 'What else do you use this garden for?' Over the course of his questioning and my answers, he established that I'd like to be able to sit outside, to have space to have friends round but to keep the upkeep of the garden low maintenance. A bit more than levelling out the garden then. All of those extras added up to my real needs.

The price added up, too.

2. Expand the prospect's real needs

This stage is a voyage of discovery for both of you. This is the opportunity to expand the scale of what you can sell to the prospect. Involve them in the expansion of these needs by couching your recommendations in open questions, such as 'What do you think about . . .?'

Going back to my garden, the contractor said, 'When we level out the garden for the table tennis table, what do you think about us making it on two levels, so you can have an area for the table tennis and a small terrace for a table and chairs for sitting outside? We can extend the tiling to make this space bigger so there will be less gardening needed.'
'Sounds great,' says me.

3. Create new needs

You've clarified the original brief. You've expanded it to increase the scope of your response. Now it's time to help the prospect by providing the added value only you can supply. This is where you ask the prospect, 'Have you considered . . .?'

In a great example of creating new needs, the contractor then said, 'I noticed when I walked through the kitchen you have a nice cooker – do you like to cook?' 'Well, not me,' I said, 'but my husband does.' The contractor then said, 'I notice you have a bit of dead space next to the shed. Have you considered adding a built-in barbecue here? We can add some shelving and a work surface and you can have a small outdoor kitchen area.' At this point he has expanded my needs to suggest something I hadn't even thought of but now I really want. I'm excited about the possibilities, I know it's going to cost more but it sounds so great, I'm going to find the money. Despite the cost coming in at 20 per cent above my original budget, I was happy to pay the premium because the contractor had given me expert advice that helped me, rather than purely answering my original brief.

There is another type of need the prospect has: 'implied' needs. These are vague or underdeveloped requirements. They are often said in passing or in conversation. To pick up on implied needs you need your radar to be on fully and to employ world-class listening skills.

The garden contractor had his radar on high alert: when I said that it was annoying the candles kept blowing out when I was sitting outside in the summer, he managed to sell me some built-in garden lighting. Another 'need' that wasn't clearly stated but was something that I was willing to spend money on.

We doubt Louisa's garden contractor had been on a sales training course in his life. He instinctively knew how to identify, expand and create new needs. He was confident that he knew more about his area of expertise than she did and therefore was able to direct the conversation to genuinely add value to her. If he had given her what she had asked for – a level garden – it's likely she would have been happy with the result, but his skill was to paint a picture of the possibilities so that she could imagine the 'opportunity outcomes'. It was this that led to the final sale, and at an increased price.

This is what our friend on the 18.05 Pullman dining service to Penzance was so good at doing. Self-employed people are often very good at all this because they *have* to be. If they lose a sale to a local competitor, it directly affects their income as they live in a finite catchment area. The ones that survive learn to be good diagnosticians very quickly.

In corporate life, where we are protected from the immediate effects of our inability to sell properly, these skills take much longer to acquire, because the financial imperative isn't there – we still get our salary at the end of the month and our children still get fed. In legal partnerships – such as the one our train-travelling solicitor friend was in – they are all self-employed in a highly competitive arena. So, of course, he had these abilities very well tuned by the end of his career.

An easy way to remember the three stages and have a helpful conversation is to think FEES.

The FEES method stands for:

Facts. Establish the perceived and actual situation: the nature of the issue or problem.

Explore the consequences and opportunities arising from these facts.

Expand the needs.

Specify the solution (or, even better, jointly create it).

Facts

You need to understand the circumstances this person is facing. By asking questions you will uncover the pertinent facts of their situation.

Do not leap straight from the facts – which describe the problem – to the solution. Do not say, 'Well, what you need is x, y and z' because they are not ready to hear this. The person you are talking with needs to understand (rationally) and feel (emotionally) what these facts mean for her circumstances or business. She needs to understand and feel what the implications of these facts going unchanged will have for her business. This is why you have the other two vital steps in the conversation structure. If you rush straight from the facts (the problem) to the solution, the price tag you put on correcting the problem has no financial context. It will appear to be a large sum of money, but set against nothing by comparison. So the answer from the client prospect will be 'no'. More work needs to be done to create the context for your eventual price proposal.

Explore

To help the person you are helping realise that they do need help, you need to explore the consequences of what a continuation of their situation actually means for them as well as the opportunities presented by taking corrective action.

For example, if the person you are talking with casually mentions that they are worried because their major brand is not always on the shelves in the supermarkets where it ought to be, you need to know numbers – you need to know the *size* of the problem.

'On average, how much below full shelf capacity are you running at?'

You establish that, on average, it's 25 per cent less present on shelf than it should be. Fact.

Now you explore the consequences of that situation if it continues.

'How many shops is that across?' you ask.

'A thousand,' comes the reply. Fact.

'How many units are sold on average per shop?'

'We would normally sell fifty units per shop per day, on average, if we are fully stocked on shelf.' Fact.

'So that's 50,000 units per day when you're fully on shelf. But you are only 75 per cent on shelf, so you are losing 12,500 sales per day. And how much do you make per unit in those supermarkets?'

'Thirty pence.' Fact.

'So, for every unit that should be there but isn't, across these thousand stores, you're losing £3,750 per day in profit.'

That's a lot of money to lose.

'If this continues, it'll cost you £26,250 in lost profits per week, £105,000 in a month and over £1,260,000 per year.'

Now you have made a relatively innocuous fact have tangible, disastrous financial repercussions. Any solution now has an opportunity cost of not putting it right. It has a context, so any price tag for correcting the situation is going to be a lot smaller than allowing the situation to continue unaltered.

You can run through this exercise in many different fields. In online businesses, where data is key to understanding customer behaviour, and where, for example, slight alterations to the online retail experience can be shown to have positive effects on generating incremental sales, the FEES approach will unlock vast amounts of potential new business.

Expand

To help reinforce the need to take action, you can examine other scenarios that might help the person see even more consequences and opportunities. For example, you could ask if outside of the top thousand stores, how many other stores carry her product. Estimate how many of those additional stores have 25 per cent *or more* out-of-stocks. If you assume that stores outside the top thousand are likely to be even less efficient at putting on shelf all the product that should be on shelf, then maybe it is prudent to assume that 30 per cent of stock that should be on shelf actually isn't. Then you perform a similar calculation to multiply the number of stores in this universe by the amount made per unit sale multiplied by the number of failed sales due to the product being 30 per cent unavailable to buy. Then gross it up to an annual figure of potential lost sales.

By now, your contact will be thanking heaven that you have come along. Without your structured analysis of the problem she mentioned quite casually, she would be haemorrhaging money in lost sales.

Specify the solution

Only now, when she can see in plain, unequivocal numbers the scale of the financial calamity across her retail portfolio, are you in a position to prescribe a solution. And you will be dying to do so. You will be dying to say, 'Here's what we need to do to correct this dire financial position.'

Don't.

Take a breath, step back and ask, 'What do *you* think you need to do to remedy this situation?'

Wait.

Hopefully, she will self-prescribe.

'We need to ascertain the exact situation. We should probably conduct a full retail audit. Then we need to put in place a retail support programme to monitor out-of-stock levels and get product from the storeroom to front of store rapidly, thereby ensuring each and every outlet runs at as near 100 per cent full stocks as possible.'

'Sounds like the perfect approach,' you say, encouragingly.

'Isn't that what your guys do?' enquires the prospect.

YES. It is *exactly* what your guys do. But before you answer the inevitable question, 'How much will that cost?', you need to repeat the size of the problem.

'OK. You are running at an average of 25 per cent out of stock in the top 1,000 stores and an average of 30 per cent out of stocks in the next 500 stores. In total, those lost sales are costing your organisation something in the region of £2 million a year, or around £39,000 per week.

'If we conducted a retail audit of a sample of 100 of the top 1,000 stores and 25 of the next 500 stores to get an accurate fix on the genuine out-of-stock situation, and then ran a store visit programme to visit each store once every three weeks for three months to get the out-of-stock situation under control, it would cost about £20,000 a week for three months (twelve weeks) which is approximately £240,000. So, the cost of putting right a £2 million problem will be 12 per cent of the lost revenue per year it is currently costing you.'

It is easy to help people, but it is not always easy to convince them they need help. Doing it in a structured way helps them understand what *not* having help might be costing them. Remember our friend the solicitor on the 18.05 Penzance dining car? Yes, him again. We told you he was good.

Remember what he did? He set up the possibility that there *might* be a problem coming to the person he was talking to. You will recall he phrased the problem as, 'There's a piece of legislation going through Parliament as a White Paper that might affect your business, so it would be worth your while to have a look into it. . .' The rest, he lets the other person fill in. Knowing that people are often quite lazy, he knows they will need help. Therefore, they request his business card and that will normally lead to a follow-up call from them to him. Notice he doesn't specify a solution or try to sell his services, because that would be too forceful and would lead to the other person shutting down the conversation. No. Far better to play it slowly and let the person arrive at the inevitable conclusion that they need expert help, at their own pace. This is where so many people, eager to get that sale, make a catastrophic mistake. The chase happens in stages. It is by nature a gradual process and the person in the driving seat cannot appear too keen or too pressurising. There is no joy in the process if it is rushed or appears to be too obvious. This is the age-old art of seduction and one false move will scupper all your hopes. Softly. Gently. Slowly. Stop selling, start helping.

CHAPTER 17

PRACTICE MAKES PERFECT

'The harder I practise, the luckier I get'
Gary Player, golfing legend

We can hear the naysayers now.

'Why waste all that time making loads of random contacts, many of whom will be useless in the long run? Surely it is better to target specific sectors, target specific companies within those sectors, find out who within those companies are the decision-makers and then target them? That way, we shrink the universe of people we need to get to know and make the whole process more scientific and easier.'

Ah. How completely rational and common-sensical. After all, why would you waste good time and good money chasing rainbows? It would be a fool's errand. And, as we saw in Chapter 13, they would be right: there *is* a place for applying filters and being a bit more selective in your targeting.

But, as we also said at the outset, there is a time and a place for discussing probabilities and for being mathematical, but you must never let up on letting *random* chemistry play its crucially important role.

You need to be conducting random human chemistry experiments all the time. Why?

1. You need to practise when it doesn't matter, before you do it when it really matters

Let's be honest: you're probably not very good at this, are you? The chasing, the 'chatting up', the getting into conversation, the networking. Most people loathe new business prospecting. They feel it is a dirty, dark art, and they shy away from doing it because they think it cheapens them. We disagree; to be effective, you need to do it *honestly* and from a place of good intent. But you do need to practise. And you need to practise as if it doesn't matter.

Why do you need to practise? Because, if you're not very good at it, and you only make the effort for a real, big name, new business prospect that your firm is genuinely dying to work with, and you screw up that one, rare opportunity, you will not only lose the sale, you will also lose your self-confidence to boot. And, possibly, your prestige in the firm or even your job.

Which brings us to why it is so important to practise as if it doesn't matter. If you use every opportunity to practise, there are no consequences if you screw it up but lots of lessons for you to learn for next time. But if you are only prospecting for companies with people who you really have to win straight away, you are putting yourself under unnecessary pressure. You will tense up, find it overwhelming and blow the opportunity. And if your highly targeted prospect list is made up of only fifty companies, that leaves only forty-nine opportunities remaining! It's too expensive to learn these skills using live ammunition! You wouldn't expect a sixteen-year-old to sit their GCSEs – exams that will determine their further educational fate – without having practised mock papers to hone their exam technique. So why do you think you'll be able to turn on the brilliance with absolutely no prior experience or dry runs to hone your own prospecting skills when it really matters and your future prosperity depends upon it?

Channel your inner Gary Player: practise, practise, practise!

It is the same with networking and prospecting. If you treat every new acquaintance as a chance to practise, you will quickly improve your ability to build rapport with people rapidly. So when that big opportunity comes by, the one you really want to impress, you will be far more capable of moving the conversation in a direction where they may invite you to help them.

You invest all this effort in practising not because you are manipulative, but because you are in the business of making friends and potentially being of use to them. The more friends you make – and the better you are at making friends – the more people will want your help and the easier it will be to get even more people to see you as a very useful friend.

2. Approach clumsily and selfishly and they will feel like prey

If, on introducing yourself to the person, you listen to what they do and then jump straight in with a sales pitch – 'Oh, we do that . . . let me tell you about it now' – you will come across as self-interested and obvious – obvious that you are after something, that you are hunting and that you have selfish motives. We have seen people try this and then, when rebuffed, instantly lose interest in the rest of the conversation. This direct approach can work in certain circumstances (for example, when there is an immediate threat or opportunity and the prospect has sincerely asked for help straight away) and in certain cultures (it is the strategy of the souk – where vendors play a numbers game to grab any opportunity walking by and move on to the next one when you wander past their market stall without buying). But most people in business don't like to think of themselves as prey; they are interested in finding out if there is mutual interest. They will give you the benefit of the doubt, but if you are only interested in their wallet, well, they will quickly see you for what you are.

3. You need to rehearse the FEES technique many times before you take it live into the field

The FEES technique is easy to understand but difficult to do when you have the smell of money in your nostrils. Like any skill that's worth acquiring, it takes time to perfect. And if you practise it live on one of your small list of crucial target companies and you fail to execute it effectively, well, you will probably never get another chance.

4. The frog that turns into a prince

You just never know which frog might turn into a prince. Random serendipity happens. Coincidence happens. Junior people become senior people. People move jobs, they move to new organisations. Things change. You change. Your product offer changes. Your business needs change. Their needs change. They know new people you don't know, who they know could use your services.

We can think of at least ten examples where business has ended up coming our way because one of these things happened. So why limit your fate to the 300 people you think you want to talk to *now*? Let's have a dose of reality here, shall we? What are the chances that you will come along at exactly the right moment and the people you have targeted will exclaim, 'Oh, thank heavens you've shown up – I have a real need for what you do right now!'? Small. By all means, try and land the big fish you know lurks across the pond in the shadows under the willow tree. But other fish will be good practice until that lucky day when your big fish decides to come out of the shadows.

5. Fish in the sea, not in a small pond

Even if you fished it brilliantly, you will get an ever-diminishing return on your investment because your contact pool will dry up. If you keep going back to the same pond of people over and over again, once you hook them (and you probably won't) you will need to keep returning to them and become over-reliant on them. We see this all the time. They become clients and then you crawl all over their organisation and win more and more business from that organisation. Which is much easier than having to go out and win new clients. They're more profitable, so we understand the temptation. You will convince yourself and your organisation that existing clients come first, and you will over-service them in an effort to cling on to them. In doing so three things will happen:

1. They start to take you for granted and drive down your price.
2. You outstay your welcome, manufacturing work to try to justify your presence and start taking on low-value work just to stop someone else getting a foot in the door. You will go down the value chain in your client's eyes.
3. You become craven and start doing what they tell you to do rather than telling them what they need to do, because you realise you are over-reliant on the income they provide. One day, they wake up and ask themselves, 'What's the point in paying these guys to do what we tell them to do? We can do that ourselves.' So, they fire you and appoint your competitor, who tells them what they need to hear, not just what they want to hear. You have nothing else in your new business pipeline because you have been putting all your eggs in this basket. Oh dear.

Always keep fishing the wide ocean of clients – keep fishing in the sea, not the pond. That way there is always stuff in the pipeline rattling down so you have plenty of conversations going on, enough of which will be getting to the point where something good will happen.

There is another advantage to behaving in this way – you become braver with your existing clients because you know there are other fish to fry. Which means you will keep on adding value to them and be able to put a premium on your advice. New clients *and* more profitable existing ones. Nirvana.

CHAPTER 18

SPEED UP THE PROCESS, BREAK THE RULES

'When Aeschines spoke they said: "How well he speaks!"
But when Demosthenes spoke, they said: "Let us march!"'
David Ogilvy

One of the best bits of business advice we were ever given was 'Be the person your dog thinks you are.'

Even if you don't own a dog, you still understand what is meant by this piece of wisdom. When the owner comes home, the dog is waiting at the door, tail wagging, pleased to see him. Because for the dog, the owner is the best thing in the world – provider of food; a fun companion; all-knowing, all-powerful master or mistress; at times playful or strict; provider of warmth and affection and discipline; clearer-upper of mess; sole source of treats and toys. The most benign, nicest being in the universe.

Be that person when you meet new people. It doesn't mean you have to smile non-stop, be insincerely positive, be worthy or holier than thou. It just means you behave openly, kindly, warmly, amusingly. And responsively.

There is a branch of the 1960s Human Potential Movement called EST (Erhard Seminars Training). It preaches that people must take extreme responsibility for themselves. They kick off the course by imposing rules on the course attendees which are designed to form a binding contract between them, the organisers, and you, the participants. They do this because of a simple observation about the way most human beings behave most of the time with all other human beings. They break their word. They lie with total impunity. Think about it. We promise stuff to others all the time:

'I'll call you.' Never do.

'Let's have lunch.' No date is set.

'I'll be there.' We aren't.

'I'll send you that article I mentioned.' It never arrives.

'Sure, I'd be happy to write a testimonial for you.' You have to chase again and again and still it never arrives, even though they said at the time you helped them out of a tight spot how immensely grateful they were to you.

Sound familiar?

We do it to ourselves even more: I'll start that diet tomorrow. I'll go running in the morning. I'll finish that report over the weekend. You get the picture.

We give our word and then fail to act on that word. We break trust when we do this and even though we usually dismiss it as trivial, as 'it's just one of those things you say', for EST disciples, your word is your bond.

Imagine a world where your word really is your bond.

Welcome to the world of new business.

How easy to differentiate yourself as a potential business partner and friend by ensuring that *whatever* you promise to *whomever* you promise it to, you always deliver – without fail.

It may well be that you are in dialogue with someone who already has in place an organisation to do for them what you do. It is unlikely you will dislodge the incumbent easily or instantly. This is a gradual process. But you will loosen the incumbent's grip on this client if you become the dynamic one in the relationship – the one waiting in the wings who is always there with a helpful hand.

Most incumbents have been in place for a while. They may have slowed down a little since they were first appointed and this provides you with an opportunity. Maybe they don't keep their word quite as assiduously as they used to, back in the early days of the relationship. Maybe they don't return calls straight away or keep strictly to deadlines or over-deliver quite like they used to. If this is the case, and it usually is, then all you have to do is be super proactive. Do all that you say you will do. On time, or preferably ahead of time. If you do this, your future client cannot help but notice the discrepancy between the efficiency of the service you are providing and the more lackadaisical standard of the incumbent. It's flattering to be paid attention and off-putting when you feel ignored or taken for granted. The art of the chase is to make the object of your affections feel special. And your job is made so much easier if the existing partner is either never available or putting their attention elsewhere.

F**k polite

In a sea of sameness, one of the most effective new business tools to deploy is having a unique tone of voice and approach to communicating with new business prospects. We are always astounded at the anodyne style of most companies' approaches to communicating with prospective clients. The most potent weapons at your disposal – the words you say and write – are squandered by so many. Meaning gets lost in jargon and three-letter acronyms. In the attempt to appear 'professional', people forget to speak and write like a human being. So if your communication is clear, concise, well phrased, insightful, honest and well reasoned, and if it plays back to the new business prospect the sentiment of what they have said they need help with and uses the language they employ, you will stand out a mile from the morass of badly written, misspelled, cut-and-paste illiterate linguini that gets served up in so much business communication.

If you combine an exquisite command of language with an elegantly simple layout and a willingness to state baldly what your honest opinion is about their problem, without wrapping it all up in sycophantic, hedge-betting, convoluted phraseology and overcomplicated process charts, graphs and clip art, you will tip the playing field massively in your favour.

The point is to be *distinctively different*. Be refreshingly candid and to the point. So many documents, emails and written communication in business are overblown, self-important, clichéd and unmemorable. If you have a blinding insight into someone's business that you wish to share, go to the effort of crafting how you express it brilliantly. Anything else is a disservice to your cleverness.

If you want to see a sea of sameness, to remind you of everything you must strive *not* to be, just read the newsfeed on LinkedIn. Read a handful of the profiles of people in your contacts. Each and every one likely contains a litany of communication sins. They're a randomised set of business buzzwords. Here's an example:

> A multifaceted, non-executive director with C-suite, blue chip executive experience, bringing devotion to customers, data, digital and brands to the top table internationally.

It reads like a pastiche of a corporate résumé. It is the sort of drivel that spews from the mouths of TV sitcom business executives when they are being satirised, without the self-awareness or irony.

Speak and write like a human being and you will stand out from the unwitting David Brent imitators around you. Like this:

I write. Four novels and hundreds of advertisements. Mainly radio ads. I also cast, produce and direct them. For this, I have won more awards than anyone else in the industry . . . three D&AD Pencils and a Lifetime Achievement Award from the Aerials. Then there's the Radio Advertising Fellowship presented at the House of Lords. Oh God, this looks so boastful but for two things:

- I am completely useless at everything else.
- If you can't boast on LinkedIn, where can you?

Human. Fallible. Self-aware. Funny and gentle. It stands out, compared to pompous, self-aggrandising and humourless copy. Who would you rather meet? If it's the portfolio NED with a penchant for worshipping customers, well, good luck to you.

The smart people stand out – they zig when everyone else is sagging (yeah, you read that right) – they don't follow the herd.

The rules are, there are no rules.

Break every rule you find. Like this:

LinkedIn message from: David Kean 12:25 PM October 30

I'm one of the people being vetted by your talent team in NYC as a candidate coach to work with you. I suspect I am breaking all sorts of protocols getting in touch with you, but I am no respecter of processes that take months to get any results and believe that the best way to see how we might work together is for us to meet face to face. I only work with top leaders who don't have the time or the inclination to prevaricate but who need an experienced and forthright person to discuss the big issues with and who won't pull his punches in helping you. I have worked with the European head of strategy for a major automotive company, the head of fixed income for a leading investment bank, and the worldwide CCO of a publicly quoted fashion giant – all people in a hurry. I was head of sales in Europe for a large communications company before setting up my own business, the Caffeine Partnership, and come from the advertising and media environment. So I understand your world as well as being able to bring in learning from elsewhere in the business world. I understand the need for someone to talk with when you have shareholders to satisfy and subordinates to lead. I can help you navigate that world and, crucially, think through decisions and help you create options, as well as resolve the demands of office and family. From what I see it would be very stimulating to work together. Would you like to meet up on your next trip to London for a coffee or discuss it all in more detail over lunch? Please forgive the direct approach – it is the way I find works best for all concerned. David

Linkedin message reply from the CEO David wanted to work with 4:38 PM October 30

David. I love the directness. It's how I operate. I'm in London Nov 5 – are you around?

This was the LinkedIn correspondence between David and a potential coaching client. Leading up to it, there had been a 'beauty parade' organised by the human resources department of the commissioning company and this department was handling the process. Only thing was, it was taking weeks for them to give any dates for a potential screening interview for each candidate coach with the HR department, let alone to speak with the actual client, the CEO.

We took a calculated risk and contacted the CEO directly. By the time the HR people had got around to fixing a telephone call to vet David, the deal was done – David and the client had already met and the client was sold on working with him. Turns out the CEO – like so many CEOs – was a man in a hurry. The HR department was staffed by people who didn't understand the meaning of the word 'hurry'. They were slow, deliberative and infuriatingly dilatory. Way too slow for the pace that the CEO operated at – he'd asked them to sort him out an executive coach the previous April.

We debated for about thirty seconds whether we should contact the CEO directly. It was a no-brainer – if we kept on plodding at the pace at which the HR people were proceeding, we'd be halfway through the following year before they got around to speaking with all the candidate coaches. We figured we had nothing to lose: if they heard we had gone over their heads, then they would probably get mildly cross with us and give us a reprimand. No big deal. And if we kept going on their timetable, we would have died of tedium. Plus, our distinctive brand persona was to be direct and unconventional. We don't play by the rules. We seek unfair competitive advantage in any competitive situation. We take calculated risks. It's what we teach and it's what we practise.

The other coaches never got a look in. This is a general rule of business, let alone new business: those who make a move usually win when in competition with those who stand still waiting and politely play by the rules.

Fine words butter no parsnips.

Use your words, your voice and your nerve to make your prospects want to march with you.

CHAPTER 19

ACE THE FIRST MEETING

'Most of us need a little preparation to
get into the mood we need'
Andy Warhol

It's happening. The efforts you've made are paying off. You've got
dates in the diary to meet, formally, with new prospects for the
first time. Suddenly it has got real: this is where you need to sell
yourself and the firm and, most importantly, establish what the
client wants, so you can move from contact to contract.

But how?

Many of us turn up to first meetings with a laptop full of
PowerPoint charts – the 'we've done all this work and you're
damn well going to see it' approach.

Or, conversely, we do it on the fly. If we're not going to cudgel
them into submission with the weight of our presentation deck
or pitch book, we're the opposite: going with the flow to see
where the conversation takes us, reacting in the moment. Best
to give some thought ahead of time. That way you ensure that
the meeting is a productive one, with a positive, tangible result.
Not a wasted opportunity over two cups of coffee and a bun in
Pret; or an-hour long, internet-assembled regurgitation of the
bleeding obvious (dressed up as 'insight') bolted on to your
excruciatingly detailed company credentials, delivered in a hot,

anonymous meeting room somewhere in the bowels of the prospect's office block, to a person who just wants this agony to end.

There's a reason the person agreed to see you. There is a reason for every briefing, meeting, presentation, encounter or interview. They have an issue, a problem. Your job is to find out what that problem or issue is. Do that and you can help them. Fail to find out and you miss your chance. So, to maximise your chances of finding out what's bothering the prospect, before you turn up, ask yourself the following questions:

What's the purpose of this meeting?

Is it an introductory meeting or are you taking a brief? What do you want to find out? What might be on the prospect's mind right now? If you can find this out ahead of the meeting, so much the better. Then you have something concrete to aim at in your preparation.

Remember, if you do find out what's bothering them ahead of time, this is only their *perception* of the problem; in the course of your questioning of them at the meeting, you will probably unearth more – new or different needs they had not thought about before or spotted.

What impression do I want to leave?

This could be an explicit message – such as 'We can help you with . . .' – or it could be implicit – that you are a great listener, you ask insightful questions or have a point of view on their business and the key issues facing it. Remember to think about how you want to make them *feel* after the meeting.

What might I be walking into?

When are we meeting – what time of day or night? Where are they coming from? How much time do we have? What will we focus on if they are running late and are pushed for time? What personality type are they and how do I need to talk and behave to generate rapport quickly? Do I know everything I need to know about them? Do I know the environment in which we are meeting? Think about the noise levels, ambience, privacy level (you may be talking about confidential matters and if you want the prospect to open up, a café isn't necessarily the best venue). Find out as much as you can in advance and try to control the environment as much as possible. In other words, like a good soldier, know the terrain – we don't want any nasty surprises that compromise the mission.

What do I want?

What would be the best result for you? What do you think is the result they are hoping to accomplish? What is likely to happen?

GETTING THE BASICS RIGHT

Introductions

When she was a child, Louisa wanted to be a number of things when she grew up: a farmer, until she found out you had to get up early *every day*; an artist, but a distinct lack of talent put paid to that; and a spy, but she can't confirm if that happened or not. Fast-forward a few decades and she recently overheard her son telling someone what she did for a living: 'She sends emails.'

Not quite the varied and dynamic portrait she'd hoped to paint as a role model to her children, but when you have one of those careers you struggle to explain to your grandmother ('I work for a strategic consultancy delivering brand-led business growth'; 'What's that dear?'), sending emails seems like a fair shortcut for now.

Granted, it might not cover quite the full range of her role and responsibilities, but it made us think about how we describe ourselves and how we are seen by others. They are often very different.

Many of us have experienced the 'creeping death' of the round-the-table introduction at the start of a meeting or presentation. You know the form:

'My name's Noel, I'm the chief operating officer for MEGACORP and I've worked here for eight years,' often delivered in a pan-faced monotone. If the first, or most senior person takes that approach, then everyone follows suit, with the result that the audience is as bored as the people saying it. By the time you've limped round the whole table, the first few people to introduce themselves are head down, back on their phone. You've lost your audience before you even start.

Introductions are the 'social glue' of business meetings. We all feel better when we know who is in the room, and it's helpful to know what they do. It's the business equivalent of the standard TV game show question to new contestants: 'Who are you and where do you come from?' – and an essential part of warming everyone up. Which is why on most TV game shows, dull-as-ditchwater contestants have their introductory opening line written for them by the show's team of scriptwriters.

But in the world of business, we give this vital opening moment minimal thought and focus on the least interesting aspect of our job: our length of service. Who cares how long you have been in your post? It only matters if you link it to something that makes your length of service relevant, such as, 'I began here as a graduate trainee and I never left. There is something uniquely familial about this firm,' or, 'I have been here twenty years; every time I tried to leave, they gave me a new challenge to keep me entertained.' Both of these throw highly relevant information out there for you to pick up: in the first instance, you are in a company that values loyalty and behaves more like a family (both with its employees and its suppliers). In the latter case, you are in front of a fairly egotistical individual, who sees himself as a problem-solver and lover of challenges. Both are useful and relevant pieces of intelligence that will allow you to adapt your presentation to reflect back to these people how you see the world in the same way they do.

If we took the same group of people and asked one of them to describe someone else in the room, they'd probably lead with something a lot more interesting than their job title. They might say this person was brilliant at strategy or an expert in algorithms, or that they keep llamas as a hobby or are incredibly reliable. It's great to be reliable, a trait that no one seems to boast about, but reliability leads to trust and to be a trusted advisor is the Holy Grail of client relationships. It means we keep our word, which is the opposite of most people. Out of all those descriptors, you'll probably remember the llamas because it's unusual. Unfortunately, it's probably not relevant to the day job. Unless you're meeting the Board of Llama International Products, in which case, knock yourself out. But what's your llama equivalent that *is* relevant?

Louisa worked in a firm where one of the new members of her team had recently arrived from the police. She'd moved from crime forensics to work in consumer public relations. She was instantly memorable in new business meetings because, apart from being great at her job, clients loved her backstory, and loved the idea of that analytical brain being applied to their business issue. She also had great anecdotes, such as how to stand so you fall backwards when you faint, rather than tipping into the body on the mortuary table. (Put your right foot a step in front of your left one, rather than standing with your feet next to each other. You're welcome.)

What's your story? Can you introduce yourself in your next prospect meeting in a way that's memorable and doesn't feel awkward? We're not looking for a monologue here, just your name, your experience and something that's relevant to the client's business (e.g. what you'll be doing in service of that client). Sounds like another missive from the Department of the Bleeding Obvious, but you'd be surprised how many people don't give any thought to this. We introduce ourselves so many times in the world of work, no wonder we can sound bored. But the prospect is hearing this for the first time. Make it interesting for them to hear and remember.

People buy conviction. Clients want certainty and fluency. If you can't even introduce yourself, it doesn't bode well for the rest of the meeting. If you're not sure what to say about yourself, ask someone else to describe you and take the good stuff from that. Or introduce each other; not only will it be more interesting content and more dramatic, it will also speak volumes for how tight-knit you are as a team. It is a good impression to make and sends a terrific signal that this will be a different sort of meeting to the one this prospect client has experienced from your competitors.

Setting the agenda

OK. You've introduced the team. Now you want to get into it. Whether it's the opening of a meeting, a presentation, a pitch, a speech or the start of a conference call or videoconference, thinking of and practising your opening will serve you well. You want to get off to a super-confident start – no one wants to hear you falter at the first hurdle. If you do, it's going to be a long old meeting.

So many people say, 'I'm OK once I get going,' but as an audience, do we really want to see and hear someone warming up in front of us? If we went to the theatre and the actors stumbled and mumbled their first lines, we wouldn't be impressed – our tickets cost a fortune and we expected more polish than that. Well, newsflash: everyone sitting around the table or on the screen in front of you has a little money meter running – the cost of their time and the office they are sitting in. And it costs a darn sight more than a ticket to a show on Broadway when you add them all up. So, you better prepare and rehearse.

When we coach individuals on improving the impact of their presentations, there is one simple technique that people love. It's the ABCD of opening the presentation.

A FOR ATTENTION

What could you say that would be a creative way to capture your audience at the outset and make them want to listen to you? It could be a question, priming our curiosity and asking something we can relate to, empathise with or would like to see answered. Or it could be a challenging statement. Or a surprising statistic or fact. Whatever it is, it should be one, crisp sentence before you move on to . . .

B FOR BENEFITS

Audiences are selfish. They want to know, 'What's in it for me?' if they listen to you. Your job here is to outline what they will gain by listening to you. What they will learn that they didn't already know? What will they do differently as a result of hearing you?

C FOR CREDENTIALS

Who are you and what gives you the right to speak on this subject? You can also include a line about your company here.

D FOR DIRECTIONS

Here's where you verbally outline the journey you'll take with your presentation, Zoom call or workshop. Audiences need the reassurance that you and they know where you are all headed, that you are responsible with their time and that there is a route map.

The trick with the ABCD device is to keep it tight. It's not about creating a dense paragraph to cover each section, it's about one sentence. Less is more.

For example:

ATTENTION: According to scientists, smartphone use has left people with such short attention spans that even a goldfish can hold a thought for longer.

BENEFIT: I'm going to give you a technique that can grab your audience's attention for longer than the average human's eight-second attention span (goldfish are believed to have an attention span of nine seconds).

CREDENTIALS: I've been helping people improve their communications impact for over two decades, working with some of the world's best public speakers and most dynamic organisations.

DIRECTION: This page will finish shortly and then you can try it out for yourself.

A NOTE ON CONFIDENCE

Louisa's first gainful employment was at the Rose and Crown pub. She spent the summer liberally garnishing sandwiches with cress. Every experience is a learning opportunity. She learned that no one likes cress.

As the opportunities for sandwich garnishing dried up like a loaf of Mother's Pride left out in the sun, she turned her attention to the corporate world. Fast-forward to 1995 and there she was, sitting in her first client meeting with her boss.

The client is the CEO of a management consultancy. Louisa and her boss are discussing media opportunities to raise the client company's profile. They've been in full flow for almost an hour, and Louisa has been following the back and forth with intense concentration. Eventually, they pause for breath and it's her time to speak. She takes a breath, opens her mouth and makes what she thinks is a cogent, salient and insightful suggestion.

The CEO literally jumps.

Louisa had been so quiet in the meeting up to that point that the CEO had forgotten she was there, and the sound of her voice made the client jump out of her skin.

Whilst that was rather an extreme reaction, and one that was dealt with in the time-honoured way of pretending it didn't happen, it's a salutary reminder that when you bring people to a meeting, make sure everyone on your team knows why they are there and what they are going to talk about. Otherwise, at best, the client forgets you are in the room and, at worst, she thinks to herself, *Why am I paying for all these people, when only half of them are making any contribution to this discussion or to my business?*

Meetings can be minefields. And for many people we work with, meetings when you're in the minority – perhaps you're a female in a predominantly male environment or a non-English speaker in a roomful of Brits – can be places where confidence goes to die. Take this example from our postbag:

I'm good at my job but my lack of confidence can be detrimental. I work in a very male environment. I don't speak up in meetings. I have a little voice which communicates the feeling that everything I suggest is stupid. I also never know when to talk. I get palpitations when I want to cut in during a group discussion, then I leave it too late and someone else says what I was thinking. And when I do talk, I think other people are bored. How can I be more relaxed, more confident and speak with authority in business situations?

That little voice in our heads has a lot to answer for. Time to turn down the volume on the incessant negative self-talk and big up yourself. Have you ever been in a meeting when someone has said something that is patently nonsense but has said it with such confidence that everyone else nods sagely at their 'wisdom'? Follow these tips and that person could be you!

Actually, no. Because this is not about who's got the loudest voice in the room or who can dominate the conversation. It's about recognising that you're in that meeting for a reason and you have every right to have a point of view and join in the debate. Yes, sometimes people will disagree with you but that's OK. Because you won't agree with everyone either. To take an RAF Bomber Command analogy from World War II: 'If you're not getting flack, you're not over the target.'

Confidence usually grows by doing things a bit differently on a daily basis, by pushing yourself out of your comfort zone and living to tell the tale. With that in mind, here are a few practical, small things that have worked for many of the professionals we know:

1. Know your stuff, especially the numbers. If you thought your days of revision ended with your last university exam, think again. Revise and rehearse your presentation so that you are on top of all the details and know it without having to read from your slides. Anyone can read from slides. You're better than that.

2. Don't wait for ages to speak up, like Louisa did in her first client meeting. Ask a question early to get your voice heard in the room. This stops you sitting there worrying about when you're going to speak.

3. Be yourself. Talk in a way that's comfortable and natural for you. Don't feel you have to act or speak like others in the room. Authentic voices get respect. And if you don't agree with what's being said, say so. Too many mistakes in life and work come from groupthink; alternative viewpoints are necessary to drive innovation and creative change. As Gandhi said: be the change you want to see.

4. Practise some positive self-talk. Remind yourself: 'I know my stuff, I am brilliant.' Even if you don't feel it, it does seem to give you the illusion of confidence that's then backed up by reality when you nail the meeting. If you're starting out, target one issue on the agenda where you express your well-researched and thoughtful point of view. Confine yourself to that and congratulate yourself when you have done it. Next time, expand a little and add to your repertoire of agenda items to comment on. Keep on adding to your expertise and viewpoint and keep on speaking up. Soon, you'll be in the habit of talking *and* being listened to, and then there will be no stopping you.

5. Warm up prior to the meeting. Go somewhere on your own (the toilets are usually empty or just find a quiet corridor) and shake your body as if you were going to do some exercise. You need to signal to your body that it's time to perform, and moving more vigorously will trigger your brain to release adrenaline, which will make you more alert and physically prepared. You will breathe more deeply, causing your body to send more oxygen to your brain, where it increases brain activity.

Pretend you have a toffee in your mouth and chew it in an exaggerated way to warm up your mouth muscles and then say out loud: 'I want to kick you!' a couple of times. This particular phrase moves all your mouth muscles and thus warms them up ready to speak in the meeting. It helps you to loosen up your throat, where your voice comes from, and hear your voice out loud as well. Most people rush from one meeting to the next. Their heads are still filled with the stuff from the last meeting they just came from, they grab a coffee, sit down and start. No wonder our experience of meetings is so mediocre. Start by getting yourself *in state*, like an athlete does, and not in a state, which is your fate if you are not mentally and physically prepared.

6. Don't hide in plain sight. Examples of this are: taking notes, making the coffee, writing the flip charts. You're in the meeting but you're not really contributing to the debate. Sit yourself in the middle of the table, take up space, get involved. Get someone else to take the notes. Even if it is your job to take the notes, that's the perfect excuse to get your voice heard in the room. You can ask for clarification on a point someone has made (so you ensure you get it down accurately), or link one person's thoughts to another issue from earlier on. If you take notes actively rather than passively, you can make connections no one else might spot.

For those of you that do like a garnish, here's a thought: stop caring so much about what people think of you and start caring more about what you think of them. It's liberating.

FIRST MEETING CHECKLIST

The biggest buy signal is when the prospect agrees to see you. It is your job to find out why that is and what their problem is. And, if you have a prospect meeting, always show up – no last-minute cancelling – and never be late. A colleague of ours has a saying he has lived by throughout his forty-year career, and he was chairman of a very successful business he built from a minnow: 'Ten minutes early is five minutes late.'

He and his team always arrive at the venue where the meeting is taking place at least fifteen minutes ahead of time. Why? Because you can relax then. There is nothing worse than stumbling into a meeting late, especially a first meeting. You are always playing catch-up and it makes an appalling first impression. Only Drivers will tell you this directly to your face, but all three other personality types will be thinking it.

An additional advantage is that whilst you are waiting, you can observe the world around you – this is useful if you are at the client's place of work. You can pick the best spot if you are meeting in a café or restaurant. You can get your head straight and run through the key points of the meeting you are about to have. You can observe the notices, photos and mission statements hung on the walls. You can talk with the receptionists and have a laugh with them. Next time you visit, you want them to recognise you by sight and you want them to think well of you because, one day, someone upstairs might ask them what you're like.

Eventually, this will all be second nature, but, as a starting point for these initial meetings, this checklist is a useful way to avoid the 'winging it' approach to business development. Unsurprisingly, the winging it method has yet to be made into a Harvard Business School case study on how to do business. Nor has the assault with a deadly weapon (your weighty credentials presentation) methodology.

1. Write down the outcomes wanted from the meeting

2. 'Needs analysis' questions to ask

What are the questions you will ask in order to find out what the client needs, in addition to what they want? Write them down. You don't need to follow them slavishly in the meeting as if you are doing an interview, but showing preparation is flattering to the prospect – it shows you are interested and that you care.

3. Something to show

What have you got that could be of interest to them? Could you leave behind an article you've written? A book you think they will find interesting? Even a book you have written. Don't rush to your laptop; talk instead. Maybe you can bring an object with you that tells a story that is relevant to their situation – perhaps the object could be one of your existing client's products to help you tell a compelling and interesting success story.

4. Anticipated customer concerns and objections

What might put them off about your company? What might they have heard about it? What could they be concerned about? What impressions might they have about your organisation? How would you respond to these questions? Anticipate their prejudices (we all have them) and plan your responses.

5. Points of difference vis-à-vis competitors

The probability is that the prospect client you are meeting with already has an advisory company working for them. It will be one of your competitors. So you need to remind the prospect why your firm is different. Never, ever, knock the competition. If you do, you are implicitly criticising the prospect client's judgement. You need credible reasons – evidence and facts – to support any claims you make. Do not start listing matters of opinion or fall back on the age-old assertion that your people are what makes the difference. It's not believable. Be more inventive than that: cite accolades, awards, testimonials, evidence that your firm has a reputation for being more effective than its rivals. Give it a unique selling proposition – give them a reason to believe you are different and better.

6. Meaningful benefits to clients

What will they really gain from working with you and your company? Is it the way you work as well as the work you do? Will they save money and time? Because we set up our consultancy using only very experienced, senior people, we could promise clients that we saved them time because we weren't learning on the job. Because we had seen many different types of problems across multiple client businesses, it meant we could reapply learning immediately into their business, thus saving them money. Make yourself meaningful – find a strength in your service and emphasise it to show how it helps the prospect either make a gain or avoid a loss, which are the only two reasons anyone on planet Earth ever buys anything.

7. Monetisation approach: investment return and analysis

Numbers are the language of business – speak fluently. Show how you are going to reduce downtime, create higher deposit interest, increase output, decrease energy usage, win the prospect more clients, generate more wheat per acre, sell their building more quickly for more money. Whatever the monetary value of using you is, make sure they know it.

8. Strategies to handle objections and eliminate prospective client concerns

You've identified what could put them off about you – level of relevant experience, cost, perceived conflict, the inertia of having to move from their existing advisor to a new one and the corresponding loss of accumulated knowledge about their business and way of working. You need to have answers to these objections. Often, objections are fired at you in the form of generalisations.

'You're too expensive.' Don't let the client get away with generalisations – you can't fight a generalisation, so you need to get them to be specific. When they get specific, you shrink the problem from a perception to an equation. And you can solve an equation.

'When you say we are too expensive, can I ask you, too expensive compared to what?' Get the client to give you a comparative. For example, what is the cost to them of not taking action? If you have taken them through your FEES process properly, this should be a well-established number by now. A number likely to be considerably higher than your fee proposal – you can even show your fee as a percentage of the costs their business is incurring if the situation you have jointly identified continues unresolved.

The point is, when objections come, they normally come as absolutes or generalisations. If you break them down into specifics, you can tackle them with comparatives or evidence. The other point about objections is that they are often phrased quite emotionally, usually aggressively or dismissively. In order to handle objections better, stay calm, ignore the emotion and stick to the facts. You will calm the atmosphere and move towards resolution if you remember that the art of handling objections is to take all the emotion out of what is being said and just focus on the salient facts.

Here's another acronym, KLIPS, to help marshal your thinking when you hear an objection:

Keep calm: It can be easy to feel defensive and respond defensively when your business expertise is questioned. Take the emotion out. Your role here is to help the prospect overcome objections thanks to your calm thoughtfulness, understanding and willingness to make it work

Listen and learn: Make the objections specific. Good questions to ask here are: 'In which particular ways don't you like the proposal?' 'Tell me which specific points are unclear to you.'

Indicate you understand: 'What I'm hearing is ...' Summarise what you think are the key objections. Check with the prospect that you have got this right.

Pause to gain control: Don't feel you have to rush to reply. Give yourself a moment to think. A pause can be very effective.

Solutions to the argument: Calmly, clearly and concisely outline your response to each objection.

If there's more than one of you in the meeting from your company, decide ahead of time which of you is going to handle the two key stages ('Indicate you understand' and 'Solutions to the argument'). Responses to objections can unravel and lose their potency if your team members are talking over each other, contradicting one another or waffling. Best to assign lead roles and who has the final say.

Objections occur because the alignment of needs is wrong – what *you* thought they needed is different from what *they* think they need. Or it could be down to misunderstanding or misinterpretation. The prospect may be unsure of the ideas or they don't understand what it is they are buying. This may be your fault or it could be theirs.

BUYING SIGNALS

What are buying signals? Only in films does the person over the table say, 'Oh my God, sign me up NOW!' The wider population will usually show interest in more subtle ways. You will observe their body language. Are they leaning in, maintaining eye contact, looking interested? Or are they distracted, eyes roving around the room, nodding and 'yepping' whenever you speak in an effort to move quickly through the discussion?

More positive buying signals are:

- When a prospect asks specific questions about your proposal – how it will work or questions about future outcomes – and engages in debate with you.
- When a prospect asks for more information and explores specific issues in depth with you.
- When a prospect praises your proposal.
- When a prospect asks your opinion.
- When a prospect objects to something in your proposal. This gives you an opportunity to overcome that objection. They are interested enough to want clarification or to test your thinking and resolve. If they have no objections or comments, there's no interest.
- When a buyer says, 'If it was your money, what would you do?'

In a meeting, it's your job to manage buying signals by listening for them in the first place. Recognise them for what they are and acknowledge them. If a person praises your proposal, thank them then ask what in particular they like so you can focus the discussion there. You can also expand on those signals, by providing more information, for example. And, if you feel that you're not getting any buying signals, you can initiate them by asking a question such as, 'Based on what you've heard so far, what do you like about this plan?'

CLOSING STRATEGIES: ASKING FOR COMMITMENT

Before you go into the meeting you need to know what you want to get out of it. It's unlikely they will buy you on the spot (they may, but it's unlikely), but would a good result be an agreement that you will write a proposal (beware of that one, remember – it can just be a polite brush-off)? Or do you want them to make an introduction? Or do you need another meeting to discuss further with them and another colleague of theirs? If you know what you want, it makes it easier to ask for it.

Too many first meetings end up being 'nice chats' with no tangible actions at the end of it. If you've heard buying signals in the meeting, you must close. You want action, so you have to close. (We covered the different types of close in Chapter 7.) There are many closing techniques ranging from the bizarre to the practical. You probably do some of these every day without thinking of them as 'closing'. But note: closing techniques only work if there is a buying signal. And try to get the one that will work most effectively with the personality type you are meeting with.

PLAN FOR SURPRISES

All this means is be flexible. Plan and you can look and be agile. For instance, what will you do if the client gives you half the time they promised you? What happens if you get fobbed off with the junior person rather than the senior lead you were expecting? (Answer: you treat them the same – you never know, it could be a test.) What if the technology fails and you can't go through your presentation? When it comes to new business, as the military put it: 'Anticipate everything, expect anything, assume nothing.'

The worst thing you can do to new prospects is fail to impress them with your preparation. Never open your notebook on a blank page. A blank page screams lack of preparation. Always have your preparation notes visible so that the prospect can see you have put thought into this meeting. Analyticals and Drivers in particular will reward you mentally for this – and punish you for turning up with a blank page.

CHAPTER 20

'VIRTUAL' NETWORKING
AND PROSPECTING

'Get used to working from home'
Zack Friedman, 'How Covid-19 will
change the future of work', *Forbes*

For many of us, when COVID-19 hit, it felt as though we went, almost overnight, from a society in which business was primarily conducted in meeting rooms, offices, coffee shops and other social spaces, at lunch in restaurants and over a 'quick drink' at the end of the day, to a world where we were all either working from home or working out how to work from home.

The pandemic put an abrupt end to the normal ways of doing business and forced radical change which has altered the workscape for good. All the usual channels for networking, prospecting and pitching were unavailable. Offices were closed, venues shut, exhibitions and conferences cancelled, trade fairs postponed, events scrapped as they all, along with presentations, discussions, meetings and pitches, migrated online. Almost the entire economy shifted online overnight.

How do you network and prospect when you are deprived of the usual means by which you make friends with strangers, with no physical arena in which serendipity can play its part? What does it mean for networking and prospecting when you can't actually *meet* someone? What if you can't have supper in the dining carriage of the London Paddington to Penzance train? What if you can't strike up a conversation with the person standing next to you in the queue for your flight? What if you can't even meet for a cup of coffee? What happens when all you can do is sit on your sofa and open your laptop?

It is an acute case of necessity being the mother of invention. Or, as the behavioural economist Rory Sutherland puts it: 'When life gives you lemons, put them in your gin and tonic.'

VIRTUAL JUST CHANGES THE FORMAT, NOT THE ESSENCE, OF NETWORKING

You have to create serendipity online.

Online networking has two fantastic advantages: firstly, its unique ability to enable you to create serendipity with millions of potential prospects. Cast your mind back to Chapter 1 and our evolutionary model of prospecting: spreading yourself as wide as possible to see which seeds germinate is, especially in times of uncertainty, the best way to create opportunity. Digital networking gives us the chance to scatter our seeds widely, to reach not just today's potential clients but tomorrow's too. Secondly, in addition to bringing the entire world to your door, you can also micro-target and create intimate serendipity with specific individuals – you can get into dialogue with them and start to catalyse at the one-to-one level. There is a myth that interactions online lose their intimacy. Whilst it is always going to be more intimate to meet someone face to face, it is perfectly possible to create deep relationships purely online. We have all now worked with clients where the entire relationship, from first meeting to concluding the project, has been conducted exclusively online. It works. We may get a bit bored of Zoom and Hangouts, etc., but they still make relationships possible.

We know entrepreneurs who have launched online-only businesses during the pandemic. For example, a creative online school which connects passionate subject experts with parents to provide online tutorial and class learning for schoolchildren on the national curriculum as well as extra-curricular topics. The founder, a mathematics fanatic, has never physically met any of the students, their parents or any of the teachers – nor have the parents or students met the teachers or each other. Nevertheless, the online school has built a community of more than two thousand families using the service, and has forged perfectly functioning, healthy relationships between students and teachers. The entire enterprise is run via Facebook, the website, email and all classes operate via Zoom using Google Classroom for written assignments. The school grows day by day as word spreads. There are thousands of enterprises in operation now which bypass the need for physical interaction. It seems you can catalyse virtually – at little cost to intimacy.

Whether online or offline, the fact of the matter is that we are dealing with people – volatile, illogical, egotistical, emotional people – so the same rules apply. There's a right way and a wrong way to do things. Remember, the cornerstone of being a great networker is not to serve your own agenda nakedly, but to be of assistance, to be of utility and help to others. Digital media is world class as a medium to let you be this. A simple example: a colleague of ours wanted advice on how to manage immigration when all her children and stepchildren had different surnames on their passports. She put out the issue online and instantly received experienced advice from her online community which she could enact immediately. In the online world, the old rule of six degrees of separation can be concertinaed into seconds. This is a very exciting development for professional catalysts!

How to engage engagingly

We think it makes sense to start with yourself. Networking online is still about building relationships, not transactions. Just as in 'real' life, it is not just about what you want, who you want to get to or get to know. Remember: networks are personal, not corporate; they are not all about quantity of connections – quality is more important. And you need to be careful not just about how you spend your time online, but also how you spend other people's time online, too.

Audit yourself:

- Who do I already know? Who do I like? Who haven't I been in touch with for too long?
- Who are my top thirty deepest connections? How can I protect and deepen them?
- What do I know (as well as who do I know)? What expertise/knowledge do I have which other people might be interested in or find useful?
- How can I best stay informed and relevant? In online networking you need to contribute to the debate, not just reach out to connect with people without offering a point of view of new information. What media tribe can I join which will top up my intellectual usefulness?
  - Tortoise Media Ltd have very well-informed think-ins on a wide range of subjects from authoritative journalists and experts which are not only interesting but are also frequented by interesting people it would be useful to get to know.
  - Politico has incisive current events and issues-based commentary
  - The School of Life has virtual classes for self-development, and the *Guardian* newspaper has masterclasses

across a wide variety of subjects in business and in other areas.

- How much time can I devote to networking online every day?
- How can I habituate my 'Hellos'? What ratios for reconnecting: one reconnection per day and one new connection? One new thing to know and read? Like, share and comment on three things a day? Do it the way you do exercise every day. Allocate a time of day and do it for twenty minutes religiously.

Golden rules:

- Don't always be asking; give too. People behave reciprocally. If they notice you are commenting on their posts and sharing their content, they will be far more open to you. Even LinkedIn, which is primarily a business platform, is still a *social* network. Usually items in which people have shared something personal, given something to the community, or told a story get the most engagement (remember, Ethos, Logos, Pathos!). Sharing other people's content gets you appreciated because it's helpful. And being helpful is what makes the networking world go round, virtually and in real life.
- Don't be just about the work all the time. Balance the business with less serious, less earnest stuff. Light-hearted is likeable online. So share information, sources, ideas.
- Be you, not an actor or 'Brand You'. If the pandemic showed us anything it is that people respond far more positively to people who let their guard down. It is usually the personal, the authentic, the vulnerable that get noticed and gain traction and followers.
- Be generous. Give knowledge selflessly. Be a 'hub' where it's not all about 'me'. Run interest groups online to discuss

specific subjects people are interested in. Spend 25 per cent of your time doing things without expecting an outcome. Once you let go of the idea of input-output, serendipity can happen.

- Try to build diversity into your network. Don't go for identikit types: it's not going to sustain you or bring different (and therefore useful) new thinking into your world.
- Aim for quality of relationships not quantity. Lord Hanson, the industrial magnate, used to say 'revenue is vanity, profit is sanity'. He thought a good management team focused on the quality of money they made (profit), not the quantity of money they made (revenue). We want profitable relationships, not just lots of them.
- Remind yourself often that you are dealing with flesh and bone. As the supreme networking academic Julia Hobsbawm wisely reminds us, it's a people-base not a database.
- Just as in real life, people like online communication to be relevant to them and timely (same as our client, Simon, said in real life back in Chapter 6). They like people who are like them, who 'get' them, who can help them. They dislike selfishness, transactionalism, feeling like they are being used, abused, stalked or ignored. They won't respond to spam, junk, overly friendly but self-interested missives, or to nakedly selling messages on the first encounter. Think of the protocols of dating, the thrill of the chase (*not* Tinder). Think about getting to know the person, just as you would in real life. Use virtual networks to get to know them, but do it subtly, thoughtfully, considerately and gradually, and try to be helpful or at least interesting. Never rush, stalk, be overfamiliar or overwhelm with a deluge of communication.

Making it all work for you

Social media works like an echo chamber. The aim is to sound similar and consistent in every medium where you appear so that all your social media exposure builds to a cumulatively consistent presence. It works most powerfully when people hear about you from people they trust and have a relationship with already. When these trusted sources introduce you, your company and your content to strangers across a wide spectrum of social media platforms, you create an ecosystem of positive endorsement. Do this and you become more credible and more visible, and more people become more inclined to listen to you, trust you and get into dialogue with you.

The number of platforms available that connect you with prospective clients and can help you to be viewed favourably by them is expanding all the time. Blogging platforms such as Medium and Substack allow you to target your activity and reach defined audiences; they also lend credibility to your content as they are both respected platforms. Mass-reach platforms such as Instagram, Twitter and LinkedIn can potentially expose you to vast numbers of people, and many businesses run very successfully by focusing on these platforms. Creating video content on YouTube and using podcasts to drive awareness and stimulate debate are still underused media by most new business prospectors. Maybe many companies are scared of being on film or recorded, but those who dare tend to win out. Video in particular is intrusive, demonstrates effort if targeted at a specific individual and helps you stand apart. And the technology is making it easier and easier to do. Contrast this with the constraints of physical venues, the expenses associated with travel, and time, and the cost of striking up first contact with strangers in the real world. Online prospecting opens up markets like nothing else you could achieve in the physical world. The big caveat to that is to remember that the best networking still has to work one to one and that there are real human beings at the other end of your communication.

The question is: Where should you focus your efforts? Luckily, there are a handful of major platforms that can deliver you a disproportionately large presence by focusing your energy in the right places. If you are starting out in business and have no 'black book' of business contacts at all, you can kick-start it very quickly by combining just a few key online platforms. If, for example, you work in selling software as a service (SAS) in the technology, financial or information sectors, all your new business generation sales effort will be conducted online. As these people are most familiar with the tools available and how best to use them, we can use them as a proxy by which to illustrate what to do.

LinkedIn, Facebook, Twitter, Instagram, Renren, WeChat, Medium, Clubhouse . . . an evolving landscape of opportunity

To create your ecosystem of trust and to both broadcast and narrowcast, you must use the different levers of social selling that are available. For example, our SAS salespeople use a combination of the main platforms and use them for different purposes. Some are more suited to media for connection and exchange, others for deep background and context.

The main platform for connecting with the majority of prospects is LinkedIn. As the world's dominant B2B social network, it is currently the best and most widely accepted medium for connecting within the world of business. In certain markets, Facebook is either an adjunct to or a replacement for Linkedin. The majority of David's Facebook connections are ex-colleagues and contacts; the minority are 'friends' in the conventional sense. Some post a lot about their business interests, mingling their personal and work lives, and are perfectly happy to do so. They allow you into their living room – a little like the business lunch where you enquire about your contact's family and share more personal information as part of the overall chat. Combine Facebook and LinkedIn sensitively and you become more human and less sterile. Like everything, the networking works best when the ecosystem overlaps and is self-reinforcing. Think of it like a giant Venn diagram: the more overlaps the better, the bigger the intersection of them all in the middle, the bigger your echo chamber and the healthier your ecosystem.

Twitter lets you join debates and get your view out there, but it is also useful to gain knowledge of the people, organisations and subjects your prospect audience are following and thinking and talking about. It might just give you an insight into what the person does in their downtime, too. Any of this information could give you a relevant 'in' to start a conversation or give some context to how that person sees the world. But be judicious with using privileged or personal information: if used clumsily to segue straight into a sale, you will get an angry response. Used well, it can show you have made the effort and done some home-work. It's the same with Instagram – another largely personal platform (with some exceptions where influencers in fashion, travel bloggers, make-over artists and a few other specialists use it professionally to build their businesses) which can be helpful to fill in the background about your prospect's interests. Again, beware of seeming like a stalker. There are also plug-in tools you can use such as LinkedIn's Sales Navigator, which gives you access to an individual's contact details. Exercise judgement: not everyone will react well to getting a sales call on their personal phone. Whether online or face to face, the watch-words are: be considered, be considerate and be relevant.

Here are four steps to social selling success:

1. Select your target audience

We've been scathing earlier in the book about targeting your prospect list too tightly as it can blind you to opportunities that are right under your nose and close down the possibility of dialogue with your customers of the future. However, with a potential catchment of millions of contacts on LinkedIn, it makes sense to instigate some sort of filter to avoid you wasting your time. Because the brutal fact is that even in your identified list of, say, 100 prospects, roughly 50 per cent of those will never buy your product or service. They just won't. Forty per cent are potential customers for your product or service, but they don't know it yet. Seven per cent of this list wants to buy, but not yet. And 3 per cent wants to buy and wants to buy now.

Your job is to find the 40 per cent of prospects who are, at best, indifferent to you, and, at worst, have never even heard of you, and move them to the stage where they are ready to have a sales conversation and are ready to buy. In doing so, you will also unearth the top 10 per cent of prospects who are already open to the possibility of buying your product or service.

By targeting your prospects, we mean looking for the job title of the person who you think is most likely to buy your services (based on the type of person that has bought them before), within the sectors that you have the most experience in, or where you think you would like to increase your sector experience by transferring skills learned elsewhere.

If you are going to give LinkedIn prospecting serious time and energy to expand your reach, it is worth becoming a member of LinkedIn Premium. You'll have to pay a monthly fee, but it will give you access to greater functionality through its Sales Navigator tool across the site.

With LinkedIn Premium, not only can you see who has been looking at your profile (don't ignore inbound interest shown in you by others), but you can also get much more specific with your outbound search terms. We often commit the horizon-limiting sin of sticking to our own backyard when it comes to prospecting, but there is a whole world out there and on LinkedIn, with multiple new potential markets for your services. Using LinkedIn Sales Navigator, you can target by size of business, by job title or position, and by variables such as who started a new role in the last ninety days.

With this type of search, you will end up with a list that is long but manageable and targeted. As a member of LinkedIn Premium, you will be allocated twenty-five InMail each month, allowing you to send emails to people with whom you are not connected. It is a good way to connect with those who are not already in your network and with whom you have no contacts in common. And if you don't use all twenty-five, the ones you haven't used roll over into the next month.

These are the people whose radar you want to be on – so you need to be posting every day. After you have been posting regularly for a while, with commentary and ideas they will find interesting and relevant based on your knowledge of their interests and what they themselves comment on, they may have become habituated to your point of view and presence. So you can email them to try to open a more personalised dialogue. Which brings us to:

2. Reach your target audience

Your first task is to try to increase your network by connecting with as many people as you can on your prospect list.

As with 'real life' prospecting, it is always easier to connect with someone where you have other contacts in common. LinkedIn makes this easy for us by stating who our mutual connections are when we click on someone's profile. Start here. But beware: the aim is not to look at your most well-connected contact and start mining their address book. Always go back to first principles: who do you genuinely think you can help? Whilst you can afford to have a longer list than you may have put together for face-to-face prospecting, still think quality over quantity. Who do you know that would be happy for you to mention their name when sending a contact request to one of their contacts?

For those contacts where you have no mutual connections you have a choice. You could do a blanket series of connect requests and see who responds. Or, you could take a bit more time, look at each person's individual profile and tailor a message that is bespoke to them. We'd always advocate a personal message over the default LinkedIn message as the latter is a wasted opportunity to show you are interesting. Tailor a short message – no one's got time for rambling essays – and make it engaging: remember that one way to differentiate yourself is to pay care and attention to the written word. Ensure there's no sales message at this point. Either way, you will get a number of people who don't reply at all, or reply months later. But many people respond quickly and accept. If they do, don't sit there congratulating yourself that you have a new contact and that your tally of connections has tipped over the thousand mark for the first time; do something. Follow up, get a dialogue going, say something interesting (about them and their company, not about yours), say how you might be of help or comment on something you may have noticed about their operation, to move yourself onto their radar permanently. Then keep the flow of communication going.

Since moving our prospecting online, we have opened up new work from markets we had never really tapped into before – Israel, Russia, Czechia, Thailand, Bulgaria – and have reached deeper into markets like the USA. We have done it by using the network of contacts we had, creating online-specific products with new pricing bands, and telling people about them. It seems that people we know are very generous about sharing our wares among their own network and giving us a resounding recommendation. And if that's true for our network, it will be true for yours, too.

3. Engage

We have a friend who is a black-cab driver in London. He's a yellow badge driver which means he's not licensed to pick up fares in Central London but he is licensed for the outer boroughs. Stratford in East London is his patch. Most days he waits by the station and travels frequent short distances dropping off visitors and locals in the area. Because he's a naturally curious person and also has the gift of the gab, he once did an experiment to see whether his talking to his customers made a difference to his tips.

On day one, he picked up his fares as usual but beyond, 'Where to, Guv?', said nothing for the duration of the journey. On day two, he picked up the same number of fares (covering roughly the same ground) but this time he started a friendly conversation with all of them.

It will probably come as no surprise to you that on day two his tips had increased by 70 per cent.

This is 'engagement' in practice. Most of us, unless we are in a foul mood or have no social skills, respond well to others taking an interest in us. Especially if that other person is upbeat, friendly and open. It's hard to continue to be a miserable sod when someone is 'relentlessly entertaining', which is, by the way, Disney's internal mantra.

Your job as a social media engagement officer is a lot easier than being a cab driver. You don't have to speak to anyone at this stage, you just have to share some information that they may find useful themselves or pass on to others they know who will find it useful.

This is where your blogs, articles, opinions, webinars, think pieces, speeches, links to online events you participated in or spoke at, or new product and initiatives news can be uploaded onto your stream for your audience to engage with. If you are regularly sharing useful, informative, stimulating content from you or your organisation, your audience will become aware of you and – if your content is decent – come to value what you provide. The more active you are, the more your profile will be visited and the more likely you are to receive a warm reception to your overtures or to be contacted directly by others.

Jonah Berger is the author of the *New York Times* bestseller, *Contagious: Why Things Catch On*, and is also a marketing professor at the Wharton School at the University of Pennsylvania. He talks about what psychologists would call a trigger – something that makes people think about it, talk about it and share it. It might be your blog. It might be your company's weekly email. Or it could be your Twitter feed. Berger has a neat phrase: 'if something is top-of-mind, it's more likely to be tip-of-tongue'. In other words, if people aren't thinking about you, they're not going to buy you. According to Berger, 80 per cent of purchase is consideration (or 'showing up', as we called it earlier).

4. Sales conversations
The ideal scenario is that when the time is right for the prospect, they will contact you because they believe that you can help. If you've done the first three stages well, this will happen. We know this because it happens to us. And it's not just with new contacts. Often, our blog or email will go out to our database and, whilst the specific subject matter may not correlate with the issues the prospect is dealing with right now, it acts as

a prompt – it's the old 'top-of-mind, tip-of-tongue' thing again – and we get a response such as, 'Great to hear from you, can we have a quick chat about something?' This often leads to business.

Once you get to this stage, whether it's a phone call or face-to-face meeting, you revert to techniques already covered and do all you can to find out what their pain is so you can propose how you can help alleviate it.

Imagination and inventiveness: video prospecting

We have all become used to video and podcast communication. Where once was the phone – the dreaded cold call device of choice – now there are a panoply of methods to contact prospects and help you to lift and separate yourself from your competitors.

We know someone whose job it is to line up meetings for the technical consultants at his digital marketing communications firm. He hears the word 'no' a lot and even gets the phone slammed down on him a fair amount too. It is the nature of the job: you don't always get people at the right time of day or purchase cycle, and people aren't waiting with open arms and ears for a cold call, however useful it may turn out to be. So our friend has turned to creating short, personalised, online videos for specific individuals about a specific problem in specific companies. The videos demonstrate areas on the person's website where, perhaps, there might be room for improvement in the user experience. In this way, he can demonstrate how better configured user experiences can lead to enhanced revenue potential and bring client success stories to life. It is any prospector's dream: the ability to show the first two stages of the FEES process – 'Facts' and 'Explain the consequences and opportunities resulting from those facts' – and set up a problem in the mind of the prospect that needs attention and is costing her money.

Each video takes approximately forty-five minutes to create using the camera on his laptop and using the rest of the screen to demonstrate the experience his prospect's customers currently enjoy and where it might be improved. Presented in a positive, friendly (but not overfamiliar) voice, and as an interesting observation rather than a definitive diagnosis, such an approach proves very alluring. It illustrates exactly the right approach to take in order to use social selling to best effect. Why? Because it is tailored, shows care, thought and effort, and because it focuses on helping solve a real business need which is costing the prospect money. What he doesn't do is ask for fifteen minutes to show his credentials. This approach works. It is more time-consuming than ploughing relentlessly through a contact database, but it is intelligent and the hit rate is far higher. And when combined with a warm introduction along the lines of '[Name of person the prospect knows and trusts] suggested you might be interested in this small piece of analysis we do on the customer experience and which I have produced for your website specifically in this three-minute video . . .', it lines up the sales conversation very nicely and with a phenomenal rate of effectiveness.

This is a brilliant example of how, once you have identified your prospect, you can engage with her in a meaningful and relevant way that elevates you above your competition. In many ways, this is the quintessential example of how to network and prospect actively using online tools.

By contrast, our friend also uses another technique we recommend when he does manage to get the follow-up conversation. He has also noticed that – surprise, surprise – he can now get business up to four times more effectively if he doesn't talk about his product at all. He just asks the prospect questions and indicates there might be merit in a more detailed chat – 'Do you have your calendar open?' And when they have the more detailed chat he asks more questions and completes the FEES process to help the prospect self-diagnose. Like any good trusted advisor, he helps the prospective client to reach the right conclusion: that something must be done about this situation. And that he is the right person to help her do that something.

The point is, there are so many channels to prospect now that a little bit of inventiveness allied to thoughtfulness and tailoring can create content of real value to help your prospect. But beware: it gets awfully crowded out there very quickly. Our Facebook feeds are choc-a-bloc with video seminar trailers offering everything from how to get rock star publicity for your blog to online 'mind valley' workshops about spiritual energy channelling. The channels of contact are more plentiful and provide scope for being bespoke and illustrating or demonstrating how you can help. So experiment. But be quick about it, be differentiated and don't be a cynical marketer.

Put the elements together, catalyse the reaction and one thing leads to another. It is the simple law of human chemistry.

A new world of possibility

The online experience cannot replicate haphazard idea generation, nor can it replace the genuine human need for physical company, connection, communal experience and touch. We are social and sociable creatures. We crave connection. Enforced social isolation and distancing has taught us valuable new digital skills, made us more creative and to be more discerning about the best use of our time. This is undeniable and important, and it has reshaped our way of doing business. The future of catalysing connections will use both real-world and online techniques. If utilised correctly, online platforms offer a fabulously valuable way to spread our network and to engage more rapidly, more frequently and more efficiently. To use both online and real-life techniques for your networking and prospecting is to use the whole chemistry set – the most powerful combination there is, *if* you do it systematically, methodically, with flair and imagination.

CHAPTER 21

FOLLOW UP OR GIVE UP?

Don Draper: 'I've left some messages for you.'
Roger Sterling: 'And I've ignored them
and that's my message for you.'
Mad Men

We met a woman from a leading engineering company at a dinner that had been laid on by a speaker bureau which was showcasing its new line-up of talent. In between the five-minute slots the speakers were given, the dinner courses arrived and we started talking. We were getting on famously. She was head of global talent, a big fish. During the course of the conversation, she let slip that she had a senior executive who was in need of executive coaching. He rumpled feathers and didn't exhibit much emotional intelligence, which was affecting his professional relationships and also impeding his promotion prospects. The conversation was discursive but we could sense the opportunity to take things further.

What followed is a salutary example of how to put a prospect off by being too pushy.

If you try to force things too far and too fast, before you have built the relationship properly, you will scare the prospect off. We went too heavy and too persistently because we sensed an opportunity and were thinking of ourselves rather than her needs. Many HR people are the Amiable personality type and they want to act with sensitivity and decorum, building consensus and making sure that the person they feel would benefit from coaching also perceives the need, and enters into it willingly.

Contrast this with the natural impatience of the new business prospector, who, upon sensing blood in the water, and often being of either the Driver or Expressive personality type, wants to move fast. Looking through our email correspondence with this person – which we won't share here for the sake of brevity – we can see it demonstrates not only what happens when Drivers or Expressives try to force the pace with people who are not of the same personality style but also how eagerness for the sale can make you tone deaf to the communication coming from your prospective client.

Within a few email replies from this client to our overtures, she becomes curt and states clearly why it is not appropriate to move at pace. In spite of the circumstantial restrictions imposed on her ability to progress the conversation, we carry on pushing – with the result that she eventually goes silent. Going silent is the Amiable's way of avoiding confrontation. She had had enough, but rather than tell us to back off, she just went into silent mode until we got the hint. Which we did. Eventually.

All of which just goes to prove that even those of us who think we catalyse well don't always get it right. The trick is to learn from your mistakes.

It is all a good reminder of two things:

1. You won't always win
2. If you overwhelm them too early rather than go at their pace, you can become a pest rather than a potential partner. Imagine buying an engagement ring after a first date. It might scare some people off.

Prospecting, as you know, is not the same as pitching where you have a defined timeline to convert a client. It can take months, sometimes a year or more before a prospect converts into a project.

There are moments where the thrill of the chase is distinctly lacking.

Then there's the lack of manners. Not you, I'm sure. And obviously not us. But lots of other people are, unfortunately, rude.

Most of us have been on the receiving end of 'Hurry up and wait' – when you respond to an urgent request (usually for a proposal) and then hear nothing. Your follow-up emails and voicemails go into a black hole. You haven't been told 'no', so you don't give up, until you eventually realise you've been business ghosted – being ignored in the hope that you'll go away. This scenario is being played out across thousands of potential transactions every day. It's done to us, and – let's admit it – sometimes we do it to others.

But how amazing it would be if we did what we said we would do? Or if we provided updates and feedback rather than ignoring things. We're not suggesting we respond to every unsolicited email – no one's got time for that. But if we've entered into a correspondence with someone, if we've asked for a proposal, some advice or an introduction, don't we owe them a response? Even if it is, 'Thanks, but no thanks.' Somehow, in The Big Twenty-first Century Book of Business Rules, it turns out that not replying means no. But you only find that out after you've followed up with an average of five emails, a couple of voicemails before you finally give up hope. What a waste of time. If you don't want to proceed, let the other party know. Then they will stop emailing you. Let us do as we would be done by and hope it catches on.

In the meantime, we must prevail. Overcome any natural impatience. Keep your interest in a prospect and be persistent (but not a pest). Be realistic about the buying signals. If the lines of communication between you both are still open but no decision has been made, it's a 'not yet', rather than a 'no'. Keep going. But if all your approaches are met with silence, after a while you may need to accept that yes, you have been 'ghosted'. Take the hint. Move on to someone who deserves you.

But when we scent the possibility of business in the air, it does something to us. It makes us overly solicitous, too keen. For too many of us, just the faintest of outside chances, the merest possibility to be in the race, seems to affect our brains. Under pressure to increase revenue for those unforgiving private equity shareholders, or desperately trying to pull in revenue for the financial year end, or needing to get back on target with one mighty financial bound, we chase after anything and everything that moves.

We become craven in pursuit of that big win. In fact, it doesn't even have to be big. Just a win. There is something about the new businessperson who just can't say 'no'. When the RFI comes in, normally, in most companies, there isn't even any debate. No one stops to think if this is the right thing to do; they just reach for the last similar RFI and start to cut and paste it into a new document. So desperate is our desire for a new mate, for the prospect of new work and more money into the corporate coffers, that we proceed on autopilot without evaluating the prospect properly, rationally or even questioning if we want them. It is the business equivalent of the randy teenager chasing any date in the hope of sex. It is not attractive, it is not wise and you might just catch something nasty.

But the key thing is – you need to know *why* you're either going to turn down a brief or go ahead. You need criteria. Here are some good criteria to think about:

- Revenue: What is the income/profit opportunity?
- Resources: Is there a high-class team ready and available to invest time into the pursuit?
- Right fit: Does the client play to your strengths?
- Right addition: Will this client expand your learning and expertise?
- Relationship: Is there a contact(s) within the client who has a favourable opinion of you?
- Romance: Does your company love this opportunity and really want the business?
- Reputation: Will this client add to your company's reputation?
- Risk: Are we going to let down existing clients by diverting resources? What is the opportunity cost of trying to win it?
- Reasons why you will win: You have a winning strategy, or at least can answer the two key questions: Why will we win? Why will we lose?

Too long a list? Try the three Fs:

- **F**ortune: A big fee earner with lots of revenue potential;
- **F**ame: A high-profile client with a level of credibility in excess of its fee potential;
- **F**un: A client your staff enjoy working with, and who feels the same way about you.

Any prospect that has any two of the three Fs is probably worth pursuing.

Being particular about whom you let into your club, and on what terms, delivers far superior results than jumping to attention for anyone who knocks on your door. People queue up to join exclusive, perceived high-value clubs. No one stands in line for the open-twenty-four-hours, greasy spoon café down the road. Be choosy. Be desirable. Be reassuringly expensive. Be a little mysterious. And then you will really enjoy the thrill of the chase, because they'll be chasing you. And that's a whole lot more fun – and another story altogether.

CHAPTER 22

SUMMARY AND WHAT TO EXPECT
FROM PARTS V AND VI

**Your job is to find out the prospect's needs,
including needs they may not know they have**

This is not about going to a meeting and trying to sell the prospect something they don't want and don't need. This is about getting them to do most of the talking, really listening to the answers and practising the FEES technique to steer the conversation to a potential solution for their issue.

Practice

No actor would turn up to the first night of a performance having not rehearsed, and yet in business we do it all the time. We expect that, despite possessing no previous experience or practice, we will be able to master the FEES technique or nail the opening to our presentation or come up with a series of insightful and relevant questions off the top of our head. Practise when the stakes are low-risk. Treat every new acquaintance as a chance to practise, whether that's nailing your elevator pitch or establishing their behavioural style. Practise the FEES technique when it is not the most important prospect for your company so you will be ready when it is. The reality is we are all practising all the time. As they say, 'Sometimes you win, some-times you learn.'

Break the rules

If you are stuck in a prospect's company 'process', think about how you could shortcut the system. If you genuinely think you can help, you don't always need to play by the book. This does involve an element of risk. It's up to you to establish whether the risk is worth it. It often is. Say what you think, not what you think they want to hear. Fawning obsequiousness and self-serving recommendations are the enemies of new business prospecting. At this stage, you haven't got the business, so what have you got to lose?

Prepare for every meeting.

Every time. From scratch. It's so tempting, when we are all so busy, to let this one slide. We convince ourselves we'll just free-form it – go with the flow. From the prospect's side, it just looks like you are unprepared. And, from the moment you step into the prospect's office, assume you are being watched and assessed. The way you speak to the receptionist, how you sit in the waiting area (are you slumped on the sofa, looking at your phone or are you sitting or standing up, looking at the company material they have helpfully left on the coffee table?). Your radar should be on from this point forward. Particularly now when so many companies have communal meeting spaces in the reception area.

We have had countless meetings where the person we are meeting for the first time has actually been observing us from a meeting they were having in the same area. But we were on the lookout for them too so were not caught unawares. Finally, if you are with a colleague in the waiting area, you are allowed to talk to them. We're not suggesting you have collective hysterics over something you saw on Twitter, but showing that you are comfortable with each other, chatty and enjoy each other's company is better than sitting in rigid silence as if you were on death row.

Do what you said you would do

The easiest and quickest way to stand out. We recently won a project with a global financial services company which resulted in us being introduced to another part of the business. The client set us a brief to which we responded two days ahead of the deadline. We heard from our original client (who had introduced us to this new team) that the team were amazed. They had deliberately put in a false deadline as they were so used to suppliers being late with their response. We were able to demonstrate that we were responsive, agile, helpful and got more work as a result.

Build relationships online as well as IRL

They reinforce each other and online you go global. But have some balance. We've all spotted the frequent posts on LinkedIn from people who spend so long on the platform you can only conclude they have no other work. It's not online at the expense of 'real life', it's about using the whole chemistry set – being systematic, methodical and using flair and imagination. However you approach networking and prospecting, be confident. Don't think of yourself as a 'supplier'. You are an expert in your field with something of value to offer.

Be persistent but not a pest; know when to quit

Be mindful of who you are dealing with. Sometimes pace and energy is required to show hunger and keenness to work on the business. Sometimes (for Amiables and Analyticals in particular) you may overwhelm them too early, rather than going at their pace.

If you're on the receiving end of being ghosted, you can try one last email to see if that will elicit a response. We have had good results with the following approach:

> It has been almost two months since I followed our meeting with a proposal for X. We've contacted you a few times to get your feedback but without any luck. As we are in the business of selling, we hope we are no slouches when it comes to picking up buying signals . . . or the lack of them. So we suspect there is no appetite to buy these sessions – which is a shame as we know for a fact that they accelerate business growth because we run them successfully all over the world for many clients with demonstrable results – and others within your firm have had a positive experience of the programme. But we would really appreciate an answer to our proposal, just so we know for sure! We are ever optimistic and would still love to demonstrate that these programmes will fulfil your brief. Please could you let us know your thinking, even if it is in the negative? We'd love to be of service to your company again.

Be the person your dog thinks you are.

Be open, kind, warm, amusing, responsive.

WHAT TO EXPECT FROM PARTS V AND VI

This is pretty much it. It is now over to you to go out and catalyse. We've provided a toolbox of checklists and charts at the end of the book along with your sixty-day plan. Get into the habit of networking and prospecting. We've given you some ideas for things to do every day, weekly and month. Now the only thing stopping you, is you.

PART V

NOW GO CATALYSE

CHAPTER 23

OVER TO YOU

'Better living through chemistry'
DuPont advertising slogan, 1935

Whether you're one of those people who skips to the end of the book to see how it ends, or if you diligently followed each chapter to its conclusion, here we all are. This book may be coming to an end, but it marks, we hope, the beginning of your new approach to networking, prospecting and business development.

We have covered a lot. Much of which we hope will inspire you, and the rest of which will help you to actually perform better from a practical perspective. But when you boil it all down, when you look at the art of business development, prospecting and networking, it is stupefyingly simple. It is about making people the subject of your study.

Each and every one of us is different. But underneath those differences, there are some common traits. Understand those traits, and people will feel you 'get' them. If they feel that you get them, they will be predisposed to listen to what you have to say and heed your advice. If they do not feel that you get them, they will either ignore you and look for someone else who does, or they will be persuaded of your advice against their better instincts and then sue you when they feel things have gone wrong.

Business development has parallels with medicine. You are often diagnosing what's in front of you. If it goes wrong, it can get ugly. Some doctors have what we call a 'bedside manner'; others do not. What we have endeavoured to demonstrate in this book is the benefit of having a good bedside manner – and also, how to do it.

'Bedside manner' is that quality which shows the patient that the doctor is sympathetic to her plight, is calming, soothing and, broadly, on her side. Bedside manner is about making the patient feel that they have a relationship with you, and that they are not merely a unit of humanity, a number or a disease that needs to be cured. But bedside manner is just a feeling, isn't it? It's not quantifiable; you can't measure its effect. It's not tangible.

Wrong. You can do both.

Wendy Levinson, a Canadian physician and academic, did a famous study which proves both the tangibility of bedside manner as well as the difference it makes. She wanted to find out why it was that some top surgeons got sued by their patients for malpractice and others didn't, when all of them had the same technical ability and skill levels. What was the difference that made the difference?

As in new business prospecting, so in patient care: small things matter. Small things make the difference. Small things such as asking 'orienting' questions to help the surgeon understand how the patient *felt* about the treatment process, and using more 'facilitation' – cues designed to get patients to talk about their concerns and express their opinions. Or simply checking that certain patients understood information or instructions. These patients felt they had been *listened to and heard*, that their concerns had counted for something. And, in addition, these physicians used appropriate humour – primary care physicians who frequently used humour were *less* likely to have been sued than those who didn't. By contrast, surgeons who were sued focused only on the technical aspects of the disease, the diagnosis and the surgical process, and didn't address the patients' feelings.

These additional activities – asking orienting questions, prompting articulation of the patients' feelings through using facilitation cues, checking patients' understanding and listening to what the patients had to say – made every consultation meeting 3.3 minutes longer than the consultations between patients and physicians who went on to be sued. The average length of a consultation with the 'technocrat' physician took 15 minutes. The consultation with a physician who had a good bedside manner, 18.3 minutes.

'By practicing a few simple communication techniques, many physicians could significantly reduce their risk for malpractice claims,' said Dr Levinson. 'More important, by learning to communicate better with patients, they could also increase patient satisfaction, improve compliance rates and thus have better biologic outcomes.'*

Fifteen minutes versus 18.3 minutes.

Those extra three minutes and twenty seconds devoted to asking how the patient feels and letting them feel heard and understood make the world of difference. As in medicine, so in business development. If you take nothing else away from this book that makes a difference to the results you generate in your own business development efforts, maybe you can keep 'The Maxims of Medicine' somewhere on your person, and get them out before you attend that next networking event or walk into that new business meeting as a quick reminder of what's important.

* Wendy Levinson et al., 'Physician–Patient Communication: the Relationship With Malpractice Claims Among Primary Care Physicians and Surgeons', *Journal of the American Medical Association* (February 1997).

THE MAXIMS OF MEDICINE
by Suzy Kassem

Before you examine the body of a patient,
Be patient to learn his story.
For once you learn his story,
You will also come to know
His body.
Before you diagnose any sickness,
Make sure there is no sickness in the mind or heart.
For the emotions in a man's moon or sun,
Can point to the sickness in
Any one of his other parts.
Before you treat a man with a condition,
Know that not all cures can heal all people.
For the chemistry that works on one patient,
May not work for the next,
Because even medicine has its own
Conditions.
Before asserting a prognosis on any patient,
Always be objective and never subjective.
For telling a man that he will win the treasure of life,
But then later discovering that he will lose,
Will harm him more than by telling him
That he may lose,
But then he wins.

This is wise counsel. The parallels with business development are self-evident and we have covered them in great detail throughout this book. That last bit, about the dangers of over-promising and under-delivering, well, that's a disease of salespeople all over the world. Find out about the person first, then their problems.

Then help them understand what's involved with putting the problem right. Don't promise gold at the end of an imaginary rainbow. Be optimistic but be realistic. After all, you want them to come back again.

If you are more about checklists than poetry or prose, here's the same information in a different form.

The best new business development is characterised by these simple principles:

- Expand your universe of contacts by re-establishing contact with lapsed relationships, asking your existing contacts to introduce you to their contacts and allowing random connections to flourish. Open doors, don't close them. Seek to widen your universe of connections before seeking to narrow it down.
- Behave like a human being – treat people considerately and kindly. It pays dividends.
- Get to know people first rather than trying to sell them your particular flavour of beans. Find out what makes them tick, what they worry about, what's important to them personally. Find out their story – remember, everyone has a story.
- Help them to reveal the pain they have. Hone your bedside manner. Ask 'orienting' questions to help you diagnose their issues more accurately and use facilitation cues to flush out how they feel about those issues. You may be able to help them with their pain by finding business problems the prospect has either seen but doesn't know how to solve, or hasn't seen, which you can alert them to.
- Stop selling, start helping.
- Do what has been agreed, always and without fail.
- Familiarity breeds favourability: the more a prospect is positively exposed to you, the better the chances of winning an assignment.

- Concentrate and dominate: focus effort, don't dissipate it. A long wish list of prospect clients increases the likelihood of nothing happening. Be purposeful. But be open to random opportunities – don't ever close them down.
- Treat every client prospect meeting as a full-blown pitch: talk about the prospect's issues and business. Don't drone on about yourself. It's all about them, stupid.
- Prove your points of difference.
- Move quickly but patiently. Be organised, disciplined and relentless. Prospecting is a long game. Just be there when the moment comes and recognise it when it does.
- Set yourself goals. Make progress every day, not in a mighty leap.
- Block time to do specific tasks, otherwise the day can run away with you, it's evening and you've done no business development.
- Reward yourself when you meet your goals.
- Celebrate the wins.

Above all, make it fun because it's a game. This is where we diverge from the world of medicine, which really can be life and death. Let's get some perspective here.

Progress is forward or onward movement towards a destination. You need to know where you're headed, otherwise how will you know when you get there? Whether your destination is meeting your sales targets or adding a specific number of new clients (or both), or just getting to know ten more new people on the planet, know what success looks like.

Like any competitive endeavour, prospecting is hard work. You can spend years chasing a prospect and you can be tempted to give up. But treat every day as training. The more you do it, the better you get. As Mia Hamm, two-time Olympic gold medallist and two-time FIFA Women's World Cup champion, said: 'I am building a fire and every day I train I add my fuel. At just the right moment, I light the match.'

See? It's all about chemistry and you are the catalyst. Go catalyse. Go change your life. And the lives of strangers – all those friends you haven't met yet. They're out there, just waiting for you.

PART VI

TOOLBOX

TOOLS TO HELP

'The best investment is in the tools of one's own trade'
Benjamin Franklin

Here's where you'll find the charts, plans, checklists and questionnaires that can help accelerate your quest to be a catalyst.

1. BEHAVIOURAL STYLE PROFILING

This questionnaire will give an insight into your behavioural style.

How it works:

There are three charts: one for your strengths, one for your weaknesses, plus a summary chart. The strengths and weaknesses charts contain twenty lines with four words per line. Choose one word on each line that you believe best describes your strengths and mark that word with an X. Keep working down the chart then do exactly the same for your weaknesses. Even if you think that none of the words describe you, pick one.

Don't overthink it and don't try to double guess what your friends or colleagues would select if they described you; this has to be the way you see yourself.

Once complete, move to the summary page. Put a cross next to each of the words you chose on the previous charts. Take your time here as the order of the words will have changed.

Add up your columns. You are likely to have two high scores and two low scores. The two highest scores are your dominant behavioural styles with your highest score your lead style.

Working from left to right on the summary sheet, the columns reveal whether you are:

Expressive, Driver, Analytical, Amiable

For more information on what that means, refer back to Chapter 7.

STRENGTHS

1		Animated		Adventurous		Analytical		Adaptable
2		Persistent		Playful		Persuasive		Peaceful
3		Submissive		Self-sacrificing		Sociable		Strong-willed
4		Considerate		Controlled		Competitive		Convincing
5		Refreshing		Respectful		Reserved		Resourceful
6		Satisfied		Sensitive		Self-reliant		Spirited
7		Planner		Patient		Positive		Promoter
8		Sure		Spontaneous		Scheduled		Shy
9		Orderly		Obliging		Outspoken		Optimistic
10		Friendly		Faithful		Funny		Forceful
11		Daring		Delightful		Diplomatic		Detailed
12		Cheerful		Consistent		Cultured		Confident
13		Idealistic		Independent		Inoffensive		Inspiring
14		Demonstrative		Decisive		Dry humour		Deep
15		Mediator		Mover		Methodical		Mixes easily
16		Thoughtful		Tenacious		Talker		Tolerant
17		Listener		Loyal		Leader		Lively
18		Satisfied		Superior		Sketcher		Sharp
19		Perfectionist		Positive		Productive		Popular
20		Bouncy		Bold		Behaved		Balanced

WEAKNESSES

21		Brassy	Bossy	Bashful	Blank
22		Undisciplined	Unsympathetic	Unenthusiastic	Unforgiving
23		Reluctant	Resentful	Resistant	Repetitious
24		Fussy	Fearful	Forgetful	Too frank
25		Impatient	Insecure	Indecisive	Interrupts
26		Unpopular	Uninvolved	Unpredictable	Unaffectionate
27		Headstrong	Haphazard	Hard to please	Hesitant
28		Plain	Pessimistic	Proud	Pragmatic
29		Angers easily	Aimless	Argumentative	Alienated
30		Naïve	Negative attitude	Nervy	Nonchalant
31		Worrier	Withdrawn	Workaholic	Wants credit
32		Too sensitive	Tactless	Timid	Talkative
33		Doubtful	Disorganised	Domineering	Depressed
34		Inconsistent	Introvert	Intolerant	Indifferent
35		Messy	Moody	Mumbles	Manipulative
36		Slow	Stubborn	Show-off	Sceptical
37		Loner	Lord over others	Lazy	Loud
38		Sluggish	Suspicious	Short-tempered	Scatterbrain
39		Revengeful	Restless	Reluctant	Rash
40		Compromising	Critical	Crafty	Changeable

Profile Summary Transfer your X's to the score sheet and add your total scores

1	Animated	Adventurous	Analytical	Adaptable
2	Playful	Persuasive	Persistent	Peaceful
3	Sociable	Strong-willed	Self-Sacrificing	Submissive
4	Convincing	Competitive	Considerate	Controlled
5	Refreshing	Resourceful	Respectful	Reserved
6	Spirited	Self-reliant	Sensitive	Satisfied
7	Promoter	Positive	Planner	Patient
8	Spontaneous	Sure	Scheduled	Shy
9	Optimistic	Outspoken	Orderly	Obliging
10	Funny	Forceful	Faithful	Friendly
11	Delightful	Daring	Detailed	Diplomatic
12	Cheerful	Confident	Cultured	Consistent
13	Inspiring	Independent	Idealistic	Inoffensive
14	Demonstrative	Decisive	Deep	Dry Humour
15	Mixes easily	Mover	Methodical	Mediator
16	Talker	Tenacious	Thoughtful	Tolerant
17	Lively	Leader	Loyal	Listener
18	Sharp	Superior	Sketcher	Satisfied
19	Positive	Productive	Perfectionist	Popular
20	Bouncy	Bold	Behaved	Balanced
21	Brassy	Bossy	Bashful	Blank
22	Undisciplined	Unsympathetic	Unforgiving	Unenthusiastic
23	Repetitious	Resistant	Resentful	Reluctant
24	Forgetful	Too frank	Fussy	Fearful
25	Interrupts	Impatient	Insecure	Indecisive
26	Unpredictable	Unaffectionate	Unpopular	Uninvolved
27	Haphazard	Headstrong	Hard to please	Hesitant
28	Pragmatic	Proud	Plain	Pessimistic
29	Angers easily	Argumentative	Alienated	Aimless
30	Nonchalant	Nervy	Negative attitude	Naïve
31	Wants credit	Workaholic	Withdrawn	Worrier
32	Talkative	Tactless	Too sensitive	Timid
33	Disorganised	Domineering	Depressed	Doubtful
34	Inconsistent	Intolerant	Introvert	Indifferent
35	Messy	Manipulative	Moody	Mumbles
36	Show-off	Stubborn	Sceptical	Slow
37	Loud	Lord over others	Loner	Lazy
38	Scatterbrain	Short-tempered	Suspicious	Sluggish
39	Restless	Rash	Revengeful	Reluctant
40	Changeable	Crafty	Critical	Compromising
	TOTAL	**TOTAL**	**TOTAL**	**TOTAL**
	EXPRESSIVE	**DRIVER**	**ANALYTICAL**	**AMIABLE**

2. OVERCOMING BARRIERS

This exercise forces you to evaluate your new business systems and practices by looking at the barriers that get in the way of doing business development better.

Use this chart to score where you are now against each of these barriers. One is low – it's not an issue – and five is high – scores here are your biggest barriers to success. Scores between these numbers will be up to you and your team to decide how urgent an issue these are depending on the weighting you put on each.

Once you've scored the barriers, the key thing is to agree what you are going to do to address these. We gave some suggestions in Chapter 9; you'll need to tailor these to your own company.

Barriers

	Lack of time	Perception that it involves cold calling	Requires skills I don't have	Requires doing new things	I will actually have to do something	Can't we hire someone else to do this?	Our culture isn't new businessy	We don't know what to do or how to do it	We have done stuff in the past, we have never done it consistently	It won't work
	Too busy working on client business	Discomfort with selling shamelessly	This isn't me	Things I don't like doing and can't be bothered to learn	The effect will be visible and measurable and I will be held to account	It's not my job	We're creatives, not sales people	Where do we start?	We have good intentions but 'life' gets in the way	What's the point?
HIGH 5										
4										
3										
2										
1 **LOW**										

3. MAP YOUR PROSPECTS

Use this chart to map your prospects against how desirable they are and whether you have any connections that could help accelerate your progress. You will have more success if you focus your efforts in the top-right square – high desirability and high connectedness.

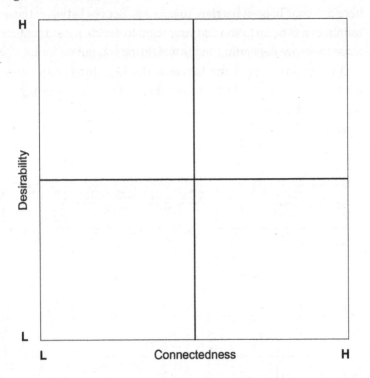

4. SIXTY-DAY PLAN – THE 'SEINFELD STRATEGY'

There is an apocryphal story of a young American comedian at the start of his career. One night, he was at the same club as global superstar Jerry Seinfeld and took the opportunity to ask Seinfeld for advice on how he could get better.

Seinfeld replied:

The way to be a better comic is to create better jokes. The way to create better jokes is to write every day. Get a big wall planner with a year on one page and hang it where you can see it. Get a big red pen. Every day you write, put a big red X over that day.

After a few days you'll have a chain. Keep going and the chain grows longer every day. You'll like seeing that chain, especially when you get a few weeks under your belt. Your only job is to not break the chain.

Notice that nothing was said about results. Nothing was said about the quality of the work. All that matters is 'not breaking the chain'.

One of the secrets of high performance is consistency. All top performers, whether they are comedians, Olympians, CEOs or artists are more consistent than the rest of us. They show up and do the work, whether they feel like it or not. They don't procrastinate, they don't make excuses. They just do it.

The 'Seinfeld Strategy' helps because it puts attention on the process rather than how you may be feeling. Your job over the next sixty days and beyond is to 'not break the chain'.

But it can be daunting to look at the billowy clean pages of a blank diary. Where to start?

Start here. Use this checklist to get yourself set up and into the habit.

Getting set up

- Identify and book yourself into the key events to be attended (virtually or otherwise) in the next sixty days (and for the whole year ahead).
- Use LinkedIn Sales Navigator to identify and set up a universe of target prospects based on the right job title and

set of responsibilities most relevant to where you could help.

- Prioritise the social media platforms you will use and the strategy for each one (for example, Twitter to comment on and share information on your specialist subject, to follow journalists and respond quickly to their requests when relevant. Use Instagram to share creative visuals and LinkedIn for written polemics and points of view). Allocate responsibilities to drive engagement and reach for each channel.
- Create your media list. Who are the business journalists who might be interested in hearing from you? What are your trade publications? Within those, who is the right person to contact?
- Create your media strategy. Who are you going to contact and when? With what information? What can you plan in advance and how will you deal with 'ad-hoc' opportunities, such as responding to the news of the day or requests from journalists via Twitter?

Everyday habits

- Tick them off on your sixty-day planner – don't break the chain.
- Share an article you like on LinkedIn that someone else wrote with two people, where it could be relevant: 'I thought this would interest you/was relevant to our last conversation . . .'
- Add five people to your personal contacts by sending a personalised invitation to connect.
- Use Sales Navigator to see who has been looking at your profile and follow up.
- Send one InMail to one of your prospects.
- Write one email or make one phone call to an old acquaintance or colleague and arrange a coffee/chat.

- Write one email or make one phone call to introduce your-self to a contact from an ex-client/colleague/someone who knows this new person.

Weekly habits

- Write (or get written) one blog per week and socialise it on your channels.
- Review progress. What approach is getting the best response? Can you do more of that whilst keeping going with your other everyday habits?

Monthly habits

Measure your progress. Each month, keep track of:

- How many new contacts you got;
- How many introductions you were given/you gave;
- How many meetings you had;
- How many proposals you wrote;
- How many new projects/clients you won.

Jerry Seinfeld has subsequently denied being the source of the 'chain'. But whether it's a true story or not, by doing a number of things day in, day out in the pursuit of new business, ultimately, you're creating new habits. As Gretchen Rubin, expert on habits and author of *Better Than Before*, said: 'Habits have a tremen-dous role to play in creating an atmosphere of growth, because they help us make consistent, reliable progress.'*

Get your planner, get your marker pen and get going.

* Rubin, G., *Better than Before. Mastering the habits of everyday life* (London: 2015).

60 Day plan

Day 1	Day 2	Day 3	Day 4	Day 5

Day 6	Day 7	Day 8	Day 9	Day 10

Day 11	Day 12	Day 13	Day 14	Day 15

Day 16	Day 17	Day 18	Day 19	Day 20

Day 21	Day 22	Day 23	Day 24	Day 25

Day 26	Day 27	Day 28	Day 29	Day 30

Day 31	Day 32	Day 33	Day 34	Day 35

Day 36	Day 37	Day 38	Day 39	Day 40

Day 41	Day 42	Day 43	Day 44	Day 45

Day 46	Day 47	Day 48	Day 49	Day 50

Day 51	Day 52	Day 53	Day 54	Day 55

Day 56	Day 57	Day 58	Day 59	Day 60

5. ASK GREAT QUESTIONS

The ability to ask great questions is a skill that can be honed with practice. Most of us stop asking questions too soon, or fail to ask enough in the first place. The quality of your questions will determine the quality and usefulness of the information you receive from the prospective client. If you are given the opportunity to ask questions, don't waste it.

Here are a few types of questions that are particularly useful.

OPEN (Cannot be answered by yes or no)	What's your biggest challenge? What does the task involve? What does success look like? What's your biggest concern? What keeps you up at night? What are your top three priorities in order? What happened: tell me how you got to this situation?
FACTUAL (To get the facts right first)	How long has this been going on? Who needs to be involved at your end? How, when and by whom will this project be signed off? What is driving the timetable? What is the deadline? What are the KPIs and your OKRs? What's the budget?
PROBING (To discover hidden needs)	Apart from what you've said, is there anything else that seems to be a problem? What else do we need to know? What have you tried so far to try to remedy this? Where do you think the answer is to be found? Have you considered [this issue/course of action]? Would it be helpful if [we discussed xyz/conducted research/involved anyone else/had our specialists look over this situation/these numbers]?

CHECKING (To see if you have understood)	Can I confirm that [this is the case/is costing your company x/there is nothing else I need to know at this stage]? Does that cover everything we have agreed? Is there anything I have missed? Is there any question I have not asked that I should have asked?
REFLECTIVE (To reflect back meaning and underlying feelings)	You seem to be saying x – could you elaborate please? Isn't this rather worrying for you? What is your personal sense of the situation? How much do you think that dissatisfaction is costing you? How is everyone on the team feeling about all of this?
OUTCOME (to establish what needs to happen)	What needs to happen for this programme to succeed? Who else should we involve/meet to make the solution the best it can be? What is the biggest thing that needs to change if we are to be successful?
CLOSED (Can only be answered by yes or no)	Does that cover everything? Have I got that right?

The aim is to keep your questions clear and concise. Bad questioning habits include:

MULTIPLE (Several questions in one)	Is the issue about employee engagement or is it training or is it planning or leadership?
LEADING (Closed questions that force the prospect to confirm your viewpoint)	Don't you think that's a rather short-sighted approach? Wouldn't you think that would only complicate matters?

If in doubt, aim to use how, what, where, which and who questions as much as possible. Channel your inner chat show host: expert hosts such as the UK's Graham Norton would say, 'Tell me about . . .' or, 'Tell me more.' Remember, he is accomplished because he has conducted meticulous research about each of his guests, so he knows where to probe to get them to tell the best stories and reveal the most interesting nuggets and secrets. You can do your research ahead of the meeting, too.

Often, the temptation is for us to go into transmit mode: trying to prove how impressive we are through talking. A truly skilled interviewer will ensure that the prospect is doing most of the talking, and that they are actively listening and asking the right questions to get the best information.

One final note on using the question 'Why?'. Of all the different question types, 'Why?' is the most dangerous. When people are asked why they did something or why they behaved in a particular way, quite often, it feels to them as if their actions or reasons for behaving in a particular way are being criticised. They can, therefore, become very defensive. After all, if someone attacks our integrity, we feel honour-bound to defend ourselves. It's only human. If you force someone into defending themselves, this will freeze the temperature of the room very quickly, and undo any rapport you may have built up in the previous time of the interview. Use 'Why?' judiciously. Or not at all.

ABOUT THE AUTHORS

Louisa Clarke is a partner at The Caffeine Partnership, a strategic consultancy that stimulates growth through brand strategy,
customer experience and employee engagement. An experienced facilitator and qualified coach with an outstanding new
business track record, Louisa regularly coaches, consults
and trains leaders and teams around the world on business
development and communication. Louisa joined The Caffeine
Partnership having been a board director at the world's most
successful PR company. A former Great Britain junior international rower and current masters rower, she brings a
competitive track record to motivate people under pressure,
understanding the power of teamwork and what's required to win.
www.thisiscaffeine.com

David Kean is a communication and business development
expert and was a co-founder of The Caffeine Partnership.
Caffeine won the inaugural 'Best growth agency' award in the
UK Art of New Business Awards. He is an acknowledged
authority on the art of pitching, and was described by British
Airways' *Business Life* magazine as 'the best pitch coach
around'. David lectures on business development, prospecting
and networking at conferences all over the world, teaches the
art of clarity in written communication through his consultancy Forthwrite, and is an executive coach to many business
leaders. He is the author of the seminal work on pitching,
Pitching to Win, and co-author of the bestselling book, *How to
Win Friends and Influence Profits*.
www.forthwrite.co.uk

INDEX